REDDCOIN

HISTORY OF THE FIRST YEAR

A DECENTRALISED CRYPTOCURRENCY
PART OF THE "ALT-ERNATIVE" BOOK SERIES

Reddcoin—History of the First Year

by Christopher P. Thompson

Book Author by Chris P. Thompson

Book Design by C. Ellis

ISBN—978-1514766521
ISBN—1514766523

REDDCOIN

HISTORY OF THE FIRST YEAR

A DECENTRALISED CRYPTOCURRENCY
PART OF THE "ALT-ERNATIVE" BOOK SERIES

CHRISTOPHER P. THOMPSON

ABOUT THE AUTHOR

Christopher Paul Thompson is an avid cryptocurrency enthusiast from the United Kingdom. Born in Bradford, UK and academically educated at the University of York (BSc Mathematics). He has been a keen follower of past and current events in the crypto space since March 2013. His first book called Cryptocurrency "The Alt-ernative" A Beginner's Reference is the first book he has ever written.

Other titles currently available:

"Peercoin—History of the First Year"

Other titles planned for release are:

"DigiByte—History of the First Year"

"Quark—History of the First Year"

"Dash—History of the First Year"

"Dogecoin—History of the First Year"

"Cryptographic Decentralised
Currencies and Assets—
The "Alt-ernative" Book"

E-mail Contact: chris_thompson25@live.co.uk
Twitter Contact: https://twitter.com/MrSilverCider

CONTENTS

CONTENTS

INTRODUCTION

Cryptocurrency was born with the advent of Bitcoin. It was first mentioned in a research paper published online titled "Bitcoin: A Peer-to-Peer Electronic Cash System" with the real name or pseudonym Satoshi Nakamoto attributed to it. This paper was published on the 31st of October 2008. About two months later on the 3rd of January 2009, the Bitcoin network protocol was launched. This technological breakthrough was the beginning of a decentralized public ledger. It allows people to send value across the globe without the permission of a third party authority.

Since then, a growing number of people around the world have been introduced to or discovered cryptocurrency. Many cryptocurrencies have been launched over the following years since the introduction of Bitcoin. The name "alternative" was given to these cryptocurrencies after Bitcoin because they were introduced, implemented and developed to be used instead of or alongside Bitcoin. One could say, a choice of brand in cryptocurrency exists. People have discovered these either through word of mouth, by accident, through personal investigation or via the media. Nevertheless, it has changed the lives of many people. It has provoked the general public into asking innumerable questions about many issues based on subjects such as economics, politics, philosophy, mathematics and so on.

In this book, I hope to give the reader insight into how one particular alternative cryptocurrency began. Reddcoin began in early 2014 as a Scrypt proof of work clone of Litecoin. This book, as well as other future books to be written on other cryptocurrencies, is a historical story of the first year. It covers the time from the initial announcement on Bitcointalk up until the blockchain had been publicly available for one year. In this case, from the 20th of January 2014 to the 2nd of February 2015. It also describes the terminology one encounters in cryptocurrency such as proof of work mining, block reward, wallets and so on.

INTRODUCTION

I chose to write about just the first year for various reasons, some of which are:

- For almost all cryptocurrencies, the first year of their existence is the most defining period.

- If I had chosen to write a full history of Reddcoin, I would be continuously playing catch up.

- Most other cryptocurrencies are not two years old yet, so I have limited the scope of all books on individual cryptocurrencies at this time.

- Currently I have a full-time job besides being a cryptocurrency author, so my time is unfortunately limited.

You may have bought this book because Reddcoin is your favourite cryptocurrency. Alternatively, you may be keen to find out how it all began. I have presented the information henceforth without going into too much technical discussion about Reddcoin. If you would like to investigate further, I recommended that you read material currently available online at the official website at www.reddcoin.com. Also, the official forum at www.reddcointalk.org has masses of information via which one can contact some of those people involved in the development of Reddcoin.

If you choose to purchase a certain amount of Reddcoin, please do not buy more than you can afford to lose.

Enjoy the book :D

WHAT IS REDDCOIN?

Reddcoin is a cryptocurrency or digital decentralised currency used via the Internet. It is described as a payment network without the need for a central authority such as a bank or other central clearing house. It allows the end user to store or transfer value anywhere in the world with the use of a personal computer, laptop or smartphone (mobile/cellphone). Cryptography has been implemented and coded into the network allowing the user to send currency through a decentralised (no centre point of failure), open source (anyone can review the code), peer-to-peer network. Cryptography also controls the creation of newly minted Reddcoin units of account, RDD.

The Reddcoin network protocol was forked from the Litecoin v0.8.6.2 open-source project. To be more specific on one of the changes made, the founder changed the total limit of the coin circulation to a much larger number (initially 105,120,000,000 instead of Litecoin's 84 million). The founder fictitiously named "ReddCoin" announced Reddcoin on the 20th of January 2014. This was six days before block number one was mined and thirteen days before the public launch of the blockchain. The general public have been able to use and mine/mint Reddcoin since the 2nd of February 2014. Only minting/staking is possible now.

On the official Reddcoin website, the community describe Reddcoin as follows:

"Reddcoin is the social currency that enriches people's social lives and makes digital currency easy for the general public. Reddcoin achieves this by integrating a digital currency platform seamlessly with all major social networks to make the process of sending and receiving money fun and rewarding for everyone."

The slogan used by the Reddcoin community to market the coin is:

"THE SOCIAL CURRENCY"

WHY USE REDDCOIN?

Like all cryptocurrencies, people have chosen to adopt Reddcoin as a medium of exchange through personal choice. An innovative feature of the coin, an affinity towards the brand or high confidence of the community could be reasons why they have done so. Key benefits of using Reddcoin are:

♦ It is a useful medium of exchange via which value can be transferred anywhere in the world for a fraction of the cost of other conventional methods such as Western Union.

♦ Reddcoin eliminates the need for a trusted third party such as a bank, clearing house or other centralised authority (e.g. PayPal). All transactions are solely from one person to another (peer-to-peer).

♦ Reddcoin has the potential to engage people worldwide who are without a bank account (unbanked).

♦ Reddcoin transactions are irreversible by design.

♦ Reddcoin is immune from the effects of hyperinflation, unlike the current fiat monetary systems around the world.

On the official Wiki site, the following is a description of Reddcoin's objective:

"The plan for Reddcoin is to essentially be the internet's official "like" button. Can you imagine being tipped on Instagram for your picture upload, on Facebook for your location check-in, on YouTube for a silly video you uploaded, on Reddit for your witty comment, etc.? Now imagine being able to exchange those Reddcoins instantly for physical goods or gift cards. Or even transferring all your Reddcoins to a game you love playing. You would be getting paid for things that take zero effort that you are probably already doing for free anyway."

IS REDDCOIN MONEY?

Money is a form of acceptable, convenient and valued medium of payment for goods and services within an economy. It allows two parties to exchange goods or services without the need to barter. This eradicates the potential situation where one party of the two may not want what the other has to offer. The main properties of money are:

- **As a medium of exchange**—money can be used as a means to buy/sell goods/services without the need to barter.

- **A unit of account**—a common measure of value wherever one is in the world.

- **Portable**—easily transferred from one party to another. The medium used can be easily carried.

- **Durable**—all units of the currency can be lost, but not destroyed.

- **Divisible**—each unit can be subdivided into smaller fractions of that unit.

- **Fungible**— each unit of account is the same as every other unit within the medium (1 RDD = 1 RDD)

- **As a store of value**—it sustains its purchasing power (what it can buy) over long periods of time.

Reddcoin easily satisfies the first six characteristics. Taking into account the last characteristic, the value of Reddcoin, like all currencies, comes from people willing to accept it as a medium of exchange for payment of goods or services. As it gets adopted by more individuals or merchants, its intrinsic value will increase accordingly.

REDDCOIN SPECIFICATION

Since the birth of Reddcoin, its coin specification has changed a few times. At the time of publication of this book, its current specification is:

Coin Symbol:	R
Unit of account:	RDD
Date of Announcement:	20th of January 2014 00:29:30 UTC
Genesis Block Generated:	21st of January 2014 5:00:00 UTC
Block Number One Generated:	26th of January 2014 21:31:34 UTC
Date of Launch:	2nd of February 2014 15:53:57 UTC
Founder:	"ReddCoin"
Lead Developer:	Laudney
Hashing Algorithm:	Scrypt
Timestamping Algorithm:	Proof of Stake Velocity (PoSV)
Address Begins With:	R
Total Coins:	~27 billion (+ ~5% annual inflation)
Block Time:	60 seconds
Difficulty Retarget Time:	60 seconds (Kimoto Gravity Well)
Coins per Block:	Random (PoSV minted)
Confirmations per Transaction:	6
Pre-mine:	5% (initially); ~20% (PoSV)

REDDCOIN MILESTONE TIMELINE

20th of January 2014	—Reddcoin announced on Bitcointalk.org.
21st of January 2014	—Genesis block generated (10,000 RDD reward).
26th of January 2014	—Block number one successfully found.
27th of January 2014	—New proposed IPCO model announced.
2nd of February 2014	—Stage one of IPCO closed at 07:59 UTC.
2nd of February 2014	—Reddcoin network protocol publicly launched.
3rd of February 2014	—Reddcoin added to Freshmarket exchange.
3rd of February 2014	—Reddcoin added to Coinmarket exchange.
3rd of February 2014	—Reddcoin added to Coin-swap exchange.
6th of February 2014	—Reddcoin v1.1 wallet client released.
8th of February 2014	—Reddcoin added to CryptX.io exchange.
9th of February 2014	—Reddcoin logo design contest began.
10th of February 2014	—Reddcoin added to Coinmarketcap.com.
16th of February 2014	—IPCO closed and the final result posted.
17th of February 2014	—Reddcoin v1.1.1 wallet client released.
20th of February 2014	—Reddcoin added to Cryptorush exchange.
24th of February 2014	—Reddcoin (REDD) added to Poloniex exchange.
25th of February 2014	—Reddcoin added to Bittrex exchange.
6th of March 2014	—Reddcoin added to Coined Up exchange.
6th of March 2014	—Reddcoin v1.1.3 wallet client released.
13th March 2014	—Reddcoin Android wallet released.
14th of March 2014	—Reddcoin added to Cryptsy exchange.
20th of March 2014	—Reddcoin added to AGX.io exchange.
21st of March 2014	—First article on www.reddheads.com published.
31st of March 2014	—Official website reddcoin.com newly designed.

REDDCOIN MILESTONE TIMELINE

6th of April 2014	—Reddcoin added to Swisscex exchange.
10th of April 2014	—Reddcoin v1.1.3.2 wallet client released.
20th of April 2014	—Reddcoin added to AllCrypt exchange.
22nd of April 2014	—Reddcoin added to Prelude by Moolah exchange.
24th of April 2014	—Reddcoin v1.1.3.3 wallet client released.
29th of April 2014	—New PoSV timestamping algorithm announced.
1st of May 2014	—Reddcoin v1.2.0.0 wallet client released.
6th of May 2014	—Reddcoin v1.04 Android wallet released.
16th of May 2014	—IPCO distribution of Reddcoin finished.
22nd of May 2014	—Reddcoin added to Coin Next exchange.
2nd of June 2014	—Reddcoin Offical "How do I buy Reddcoin" video published on YouTube.
8th of June 2014	—First phase of PoSV internal testing completed.
10th of June 2014	—Reddcoin v1.2.1.0 wallet client released.
14th of June 2014	—Next generation social wallet announced.
23rd of June 2014	—First PoSV block successfully found on testnet.
6th of July 2014	—Proof of Stake Velocity public alpha released.
17th of July 2014	—Reddcoin added to Bleutrade exchange.
18th of July 2014	—Reddcoin added to Mintpal exchange.
19th of July 2014	—Final Proof of Work block halving occurred.
20th of July 2014	—Cryptsy listed the trading pair RDD/USD.
23rd of July 2014	—Reddcoin v1.3.0.0 wallet client released.
27th of July 2014	—All time high of Reddcoin market cap in 2014.
29th of July 2014	—Reddcoin added to Allcoin exchange.
29th of July 2014	—All exchanges confirmed upgrade to v1.3.0.0.

REDDCOIN MILESTONE TIMELINE

1st of August 2014	—Reddcoin roadmap published.
2nd of August 2014	—PoSV began (block number 260,800)
2nd of August 2014	—Official PoSV video was published on YouTube.
2nd of August 2014	—Reddcoin v1.3.1.0 wallet client released.
7th of August 2014	—Reddcoin v1.0.0 social wallet released.
25th August 2014	—Reddcoin v1.1.0 social wallet released
27th of August 2014	—Reddcoin v1.3.1.2 qt wallet client released.
27th of August 2014	—Reddcoin v1.1.1 social wallet released.
31st of August 2014	—Reddcoin wiki site development announced.
6th of September 2014	—Social X details announced.
21st of September 2014	—Reddcoin v1.4 qt wallet client released.
23rd of September 2014	—Reddcoin went live on pock.io gift card service.
29th of September 2014	—Reddheads Facebook and Twitter pages created.
2nd of October 2014	—Reddcoin added to CCEDK exchange.
2nd of October 2014	—Official Reddcoin Block Explorer launched.
8th of October 2014	—Issue one of the Reddcoin Newsletter was published.
10th of October 2014	—Reddcoin v1.4.0 social wallet released.
14th of October 2014	—Reddheads newsletter issue two.
19th of October 2014	—Reddcoin wiki site ready.
20th of October 2014	—Reddcoin Ltd founded as a legal entity.
22nd of October 2014	—Reddheads newsletter issue three.
29th of October 2014	—Reddheads newsletter issue four.
5th of November 2014	—Reddheads newsletter issue five.
7th of November 2014	—Cryptofilio began Reddcoin support.
12th of November 2014	—Reddheads newsletter issue six.

REDDCOIN MILESTONE TIMELINE

19th of November 2014	—Reddheads newsletter issue seven.
19th of November 2014	—Reddcoin only e-com store launched.
26th of November 2014	—Reddheads newsletter issue eight.
2nd of December 2014	—Preview of the browser wallet uploaded to YouTube.
3rd of December 2014	—Reddheads newsletter issue nine.
7th of December 2014	—Reddcoin added to Cryptopia exchange.
10th of December 2014	—Reddheads newsletter issue ten.
14th of December 2014	—Reddcointalk.org official forum launched.
15th of December 2014	—Reddcoin Bitcointalk official forum closed.
17th of December 2014	—Reddheads newsletter issue eleven (newsletter 1).
24th of December 2014	—Reddcoin added to Shape Shift platform.
25th of December 2014	—Beta version of browser wallet released.
26th of December 2014	—Reddcoin added to Cryptoine exchange.

YEAR 2015

7th of January 2015	—Reddheads newsletter issue twelve (newsletter 2).
12th of January 2015	—Reddcoin v1.4.1.0 qt wallet client released.
14th of January 2015	—Reddcoin social wallet source code now open source.
14th of January 2015	—Reddheads newsletter issue thirteen (newsletter 3).
16th of January 2015	—Reddcoin Ltd announced.
21st of January 2015	—Reddheads newsletter issue fourteen (newsletter 4).
26th of January 2015	—Reddcoin blockchain officially one year old.
28th of January 2015	—Reddheads newsletter issue fifteen (newsletter 5).
2nd of February 2015	—Reddcoin added to Comkort exchange.
2nd of February 2015	—Reddcoin one year anniversary since public launch.

PROOF OF WORK MINING

Proof of work mining is a competitive computerised process which helps to maintain and secure the blockchain in such a way as to verify transactions and prevent double spending. It was used in Reddcoin as a means to build up the initial coin circulation until it ceased on the 2nd of August 2014.

In the general sense of cryptocurrency, those who participate in the activity of mining are called miners. They are general members of the cryptocurrency community who dedicate processing power (hash) of their computers towards solving highly complex mathematical problems and verifying transactions. This process upholds the integrity and security of the network. As such, miners are described as protectors of the network. Each transaction (held within a certain block) is validated before adding it to the blockchain. By doing this, they are rewarded (as an incentive) with newly generated mined coins or transaction fees. These coins are issued by the software in a transparent and predictable way outside of the control of its founders and developers. A miner can be based anywhere in the world as long as they have an internet connection, sufficient knowledge of how one mines and the hardware/software required to do so.

Miners use GPUs (Graphical Processing Units) or CPUs (Central Processing Units) to process transactions by hashing. Also, Application Specific Integrated Circuits (ASICs) allow miners to use customised hardware for faster and lower power mining.

Reddcoin is currently a purely staked cryptocurrency using the timestamping algorithm called PoSV (see page 25). Users of the wallet client software actively hold and transfer RDD which help to secure the network protocol. This alternative way is universally regarded as more environmentally friendly because PoW mining consumes vast amounts of electricity (see page 30 for more information).

INITIAL BLOCK DISTRIBUTION TABLE

Before the announcement on the 26th of January 2014 at 21:47:12 UTC, the scheduled block distribution was initially set to produce a fixed limit of 105,120,000,000 RDD. Half the planned coin supply would have been generated in the first 365 days. The IPCO percentage was set at 3% initially (3,153,600,000 RDD). Reddcoin was originally a Scrypt proof of work cryptocurrency.

Blocks	Reward	Total Coins		Initial block date
525,600	100,000	52,560,000,000	52,560,000,000.00	~2nd Feb 2014
525,600	50,000	26,280,000,000	78,840,000,000.00	~2nd Feb 2015
525,600	25,000	13,140,000,000	91,980,000,000.00	~2nd Feb 2016
525,600	12,500	6,570,000,000	98,550,000,000.00	~1st Feb 2017
525,600	6,250	3,285,000,000	101,835,000,000.00	~1st Feb 2018
525,600	3,125	1,642,500,000	103,477,500,000.00	~1st Feb 2019
525,600	1,562.5	821,250,000	104,298,750,000.00	~1st Feb 2020
525,600	781.25	410,625,000	104,709,375,000.00	~31st Jan 2021
525,600	390.625	205,312,500	104,914,687,500.00	~31st Jan 2022
——-	—————	——————	—————————-	—————
525,600	0.762939453	401,000.9766	105,119,598,999.02	~29th Jan 2031
525,600	0.381469727	200,500.4883	105,119,799,499.51	~29th Jan 2032
525,600	0.190734863	100,250.2441	105,119,899,749.76	~28th Jan 2033
525,600	0.095367432	50,125.12207	105,119,949,874.88	~28th Jan 2034
525,600	0.047683716	25,062.56104	105,119,974,937.44	~28th Jan 2035
525,600	0.023841858	12,531.28052	105,119,987,468.72	~28th Jan 2036
525,600	0.011920929	6,265.640259	105,119,993,734.36	~27th Jan 2037

Initial specifications of the network protocol were:

- A sixty second block time and sixty second difficulty re-targeting time.

- An initial block reward of 100,000 RDD.

- Block reward halves each time 525,600 blocks are surpassed.

- Coin circulation tends towards a cap of 105.12 billion.

REDDCOIN BLOCKCHAIN

Every cryptocurrency has a corresponding blockchain within its decentralised network protocol. Reddcoin is no different in this sense. A blockchain is simply described as a general public ledger of all transactions and blocks ever executed since the very first block. In addition, it continuously updates in real time each time a new block is successfully mined or minted. Blocks enter the blockchain in such a manner that each block contains the hash of the previous one. It is therefore utterly resistant to modification along the chain since each block is related to the prior one. Consequently, the problem of doubling-spending is solved.

As a means for the general public to view the blockchain, web developers have created block explorers. The first block explorer for Reddcoin was announced slightly after the public launch of the blockchain on the 2nd of February 2014 by user "candidakefyr". It was made available online via the URL link http://cryptexplorer.com/chain/ReddCoin. This page no longer exists.

Since the inception of the first block explorer, other websites have been created. Currently available explorers include the following:

- https://bitinfocharts.com/reddcoin/explorer/;

- http://live.reddcoin.com/;

- https://bchain.info/RDD/;

- https://prohashing.com/explorer/Reddcoin/charts.html/;

By visiting and browsing these explorer sites, only the second one is specifically for Reddcoin. It is the official block explorer of Reddcoin. One can easily access the site by visiting the official Reddcoin website and then clicking on the "Explorer" tab at the top of the homepage.

REDDCOIN BLOCKCHAIN

Block explorers tend to present different layouts, statistics and charts. Some are more extensive in terms of the information given. Some statistics include:

- **Height of block** —the block number of the network.

- **Time of block** —the time at which the block was timestamped to the blockchain.

- **Transactions** —the number of transactions in that particular block.

- **Total Sent** —the total amount of cryptocurrency sent in that particular block.

- **Block Reward** —how many coins were generated in the block (added to overall coin circulation).

It is also possible to find out the type of block generated. That is, whether a certain generated block was either proof of work or proof of stake. Below is a screenshot of block number one from the block explorer at http://live.reddcoin.com:

Block #1

BlockHash 9f1f5a21034ef45bf096da7a1ede1d9cc2f6d2e80013781969fc01d8acdcb0e2

Summary

Number Of Transactions	1	Difficulty	0.00024414
Height	1 (Mainchain)	Bits	1e0fffff
Block Type	PoW	Size (bytes)	185
Block Reward	545000000 RDD	Version	2
Timestamp	Jan 26, 2014 9:31:34 PM	Nonce	18480
Merkle Root	ea8cf6481172788571054911b1ffc4	Next Block	2
Previous Block	0		

FINAL BLOCK DISTRIBUTION TABLE

As detailed in the upcoming history chapters of this book, the block reward schedule of Reddcoin changed a few times. On the 1st of May, the projected coin circulation cap changed from 108,946,710,000 RDD to 27,946,710,000 RDD. All proof of work mining of blocks ceased on the 2nd of August at block number 260,799. A total of 26,956,710,000 RDD had been mined via proof of work mining.

On the 29th of June 2015 at 11:00 UTC, the number of Reddcoin that had been generated stood at 27,667,805,570.51763 RDD according to http:/ live.reddcoin.com/. This was an increase of about 2.6379% (<5%) since the 2nd of August 2014 at 17:20 UTC.

Since the 23rd of July 2014, the block reward schedule has been permanently set:

Block Phase	Block Number	Block Reward	Date of Initial Block	Expected Coins Produced	Cumulative Coin Total
Genesis Block	0	10,000			10,000
IPCO Pre-mine	1-10	545,000,000		5,450,000,000	5,450,010,000
Bonus Reward 1	11-9,999	300,000	02/02/2014	2,996,700,000	8,446,710,000
Bonus Reward 2	10,000-19,999	200,000	09/02/2014	2,000,000,000	10,446,710,000
Bonus Reward 3	20,000-29,999	150,000	16/02/2014	1,500,000,000	11,946,710,000
	30,000-139,999	100,000	23/02/2014	11,000,000,000	22,946,710,000
First Halving	140,000-189,999	50,000	11/05/2014	2,500,000,000	25,446,710,000
Second Halving	190,000-239,999	25,000	14/06/2014	1,250,000,000	26,696,710,000
Third Halving	240,000-260,799	12,500	19/07/2014	260,000,000	26,956,710,000
PoSV Phase	260,800-				

A projection was made in 2014 that approximately 30,000,000,000 coins will be reached by January 1, 2016. This does not look possible anymore.

PROOF OF STAKE VELOCITY (PoSV)

Instead of simply adopting the usual proof of stake timestamping algorithm derived from Peercoin, the developers of Reddcoin chose to create their own timestamping algorithm. This unique and innovative algorithm was given the name "Proof of Stake Velocity". It still serves its purpose by securing the network protocol and validating transactions. At the time of its announcement on the 29th of April, the Reddcoin Core Team described it as "the biggest milestone in Reddcoin history to date". Members of the community looked forward to its introduction.

In simple terms, proof of stake velocity was designed, and henceforth implemented into the to Reddcoin protocol, in order to encourage both the ownership (stake) and activity (velocity) of Reddcoin. The developers saw inherent drawbacks with proof of work and proof of stake derived from Bitcoin and Peercoin respectively. In the case of proof of work, the high cost of electricity required to secure the network and the monopolisation of mining power in few hands were referred to as major disadvantages. Proof of stake had gone a step forward to rectify these concerns, but it also has its own pitfalls. These are:

- A purely proof of stake coin encourages hoarding.

- A purely proof of stake coin fails in its ability to fairly distribute the coins.

Members of the Reddcoin community had to wait until the 23rd of July for the necessary PoSV wallet client. All users and exchanges had to upgrade to this client (version 1.3.0.0) before block number 260,800 on the 2nd of August 2014.

This book refrains from a technical description of PoSV. Nevertheless, the white design paper titled "Proof of Stake Velocity: Building the Social Currency of the Digital Age" was published in April 2014. It is included in the appendix. It goes into a more detailed discussion about why the developers chose to implement it.

BLOCK TIME OF REDDCOIN

The block time is the average time taken for the network to successfully generate a certain block either by proof of work or proof of stake. Both the reward and time of all blocks generated dictate how the circulation of coins grows over time.

Since the public launch of the blockchain on the 2nd of February 2014, the average block takes about sixty seconds to generate a certain number of RDD unit of account. From the 16th of February to the 16th of May 2014, RDD were distributed to 386 IPCO investors. Since PoSV began on the 2nd of August 2014, a total of 711,095,570.51763 RDD have been staked (at 11:00 UTC on the 29th of June 2015).

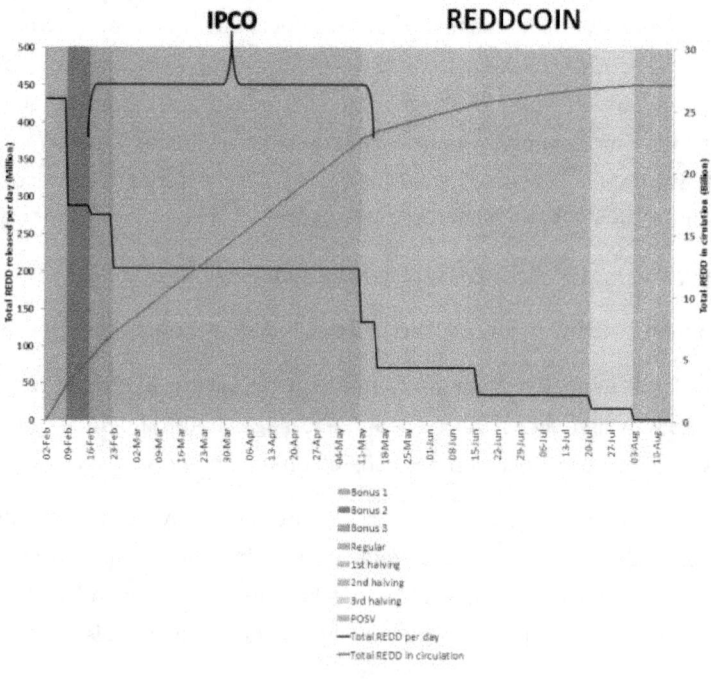

REDDCOIN WALLETS

A wallet is basically a piece of software that can be used on a personal computer, tablet or smartphone. It allows users to store Reddcoins as well as execute transfers of RDD with other users. Alternatively, it can be described as a means to access the coins from the inseparable blockchain (public transaction ledger). The wallet cryptographically generates and holds the public and private keys necessary to make these transactions possible. The software can be accessed, downloaded and installed from the official page:

- https://wallet.reddcoin.com/

Reddcoin wallets have been developed to work on the operating systems Windows, Mac OS X and Linux. Currently there are three types of wallet available to the community. These are:

- **Traditional wallet client**   —This is the Reddcoin Core v1.4.1.0 standard qt wallet.

- **Social wallet (ReddWallet)**   —The developers improved upon the above client by adding several new features to the software. The wallet provides various social features including IRC chat for official channel #Reddcoin, /u/reddcoin news feeds and Twitter news feeds.

- **Android wallet**   —This wallet allows the user to easily store their coins on their smartphone device. They can therefore pay for goods and services on the go.

FIRST YEAR REDDCOIN EXCHANGES

Name of Exchange	Trading Against	Status	Date Added
Fresh Market		CLOSED	~3rd of February 2014
Coin Market		CLOSED	~3rd of February 2014
Coin-Swap		CLOSED	~3rd of February 2014
CryptX.io		CLOSED	~8th of February 2014
Cryptorush.in		CLOSED	~20th of February 2014
Poloniex	BTC	ACTIVE	~24th of February 2014
Bittrex	BTC	ACTIVE	~28th of February 2014
Coined Up		CLOSED	~6th of March 2014
Pmtocoins		CLOSED	~8th of March 2014
Cryptsy	BTC, USD, LTC and XRP	ACTIVE	~14th of March 2014
AGX.io		CLOSED	~20th of March 2014
Swisscex		CLOSED	~6th of April 2014
AllCrypt		CLOSED	~20th of April 2014
Prelude		CLOSED	~22nd of April 2014
Coin Next		CLOSED	~22nd of May 2014
Bleutrade	BTC, USD, LTC and DOGE	ATIVE	~17th of July 2014
Mintpal		CLOSED	~18th of July 2014
AllCoin	BTC	ACTIVE	~29th of July 2014
CCEDK	BTC, LTC, PPC and others	ACTIVE	~2nd of October 2014
Cryptopia	BTC, LTC, DOGE and others	ACTIVE	~7th of December 2014
Cryptoine		CLOSED	~26th of December 2014
Comkort	BTC, USD, LTC and DOGE	ACTIVE	~2nd of February 2015

CURRENT REDDCOIN EXCHANGES

A total of twenty two cryptocurrency exchanges added Reddcoin to their platforms up until the 2nd of February 2015. Fourteen of these have since closed down due to server problems, hackings or other dubious activities.

As of the 29th of June 2015, there are seven known exchanges actively trading Reddcoin. These are:

- Poloniex —https://poloniex.com/exchange#btc_rdd

- Bittrex —https://bittrex.com/Market/Index?MarketName=BTC-RDD

- Cryptsy —https://www.cryptsy.com/markets/view/RDD_BTC

- Bleutrade —https://bleutrade.com/exchange/RDD/BTC

- AllCoin —https://www.allcoin.com/trade/RDD_BTC

- Cryptopia —https://www.cryptopia.co.nz/Exchange?market=RDD_BTC

- Comkort* —https://comkort.com/trade/rdd_btc

Comkort will close its doors on the 20th of July 2015.

A cryptocurrency exchange is a site on which registered users can buy or sell Reddcoin against BTC, LTC, USD and so on. Some exchanges require users to fully register by submitting certain documentation including proof of identity and address. On the other hand, most exchanges only require users to register with a simple username and password with the use of a currently held e-mail account.

As is evident throughout the history of Reddcoin, the vast majority of daily trading has occurred on Crypsty. This continues to be the case at the date of publication of this book.

WHAT IS PROOF OF WORK/STAKE?

Proof of work and proof of stake are both referred to collectively as timestamping methods. They are the methods used to secure the network protocol of a certain cryptocurrency in order to sustain decentralisation and validate transactions. Therefore, no third party needs to be trusted to verify and then add transactions the blockchain.

Proof of work mining is currently used in the decentralised network protocol of Bitcoin thanks to the research by Satoshi Nakamoto. Miners commit the processing (hashing) power of their computers towards successfully finding blocks either individually or as part of a group with other miners (mining pool). As the cumulative hash of the network increases, the network becomes more secure.

Proof of stake was independently discovered by Sunny King after he studied the work of Nakamoto. It was introduced into Peercoin alongside proof of work on the 19th of August 2012. Users of the wallet client help to secure the network by keeping their clients active. When coins arrive in a given wallet address, they begin to age. ...

Proof of stake is widely accepted as the environmentally friendly way to timestamp transactions to the blockchain instead of the high energy cost of proof of work.

Many other coins have implemented proof of stake into their network protocols since its introduction. Novacoin was the first cryptocurrency to adopt proof of stake into their network protocol on the 9th of February 2013.

In 2014, the developers of Reddcoin built an innovative timestamping algorithm of their own called Proof of Stake Velocity.

REDDCOIN COMMUNITY

A community is a social unit or network that shares common values and goals. It derives from the Old French word "comuntee". This, in turn, originates from "communitas" in Latin (communis; things held in common). Reddcoin has a community consisting of an innumerable number of individuals who have the coin's well being and future goal at heart. These individuals almost always prefer fictitious names with optional corresponding "avatars". Most notable individuals in the community are Laudney, Reddibrek, Bigreddmachine and Raid5.

At the time of publication, there are social media sites on which discussion and development of Reddcoin take place. These are:

- **Facebook**   -   https://www.facebook.com/reddcoin

- **Google +**   -   https://plus.google.com/+ReddcoinOfficial/videos

- **Official Forum**   -   https://www.reddcointalk.org

- **Reddit**   -   https://www.reddit.com/r/reddcoin

- **Twitter**   -   https://twitter.com/reddcoin

In addition to these, there is a community news blog on which some team members post regular articles about Reddcoin. This was created in the middle of March 2014. On the 21st March 2014, Melissa posted the first article titled "What is Cryptocurrency and Why Should Mums and Dads care?" on there:

- **Community site**   -   https://www.reddheads.com/

In essence, the community surrounding and participating in the development of Reddcoin is the backbone of the coin. Without a following, the prospects of future adoption and utilisation are starkly limited. Reddcoin belongs to all those who use it, not just to the founder who initially created it.

FIRST YEAR HISTORY OF REDDCOIN

LIST OF CHAPTERS

THE BIRTH OF REDDCOIN ON BITCOINTALK

JANUARY 2014

I.   Bitcointalk forum thread created for Reddcoin.

II.   Official website already available at www.reddcoin.com.

III. Block distribution schedule modified.

IV.   New IPCO model proposed and implemented.

V.   First Reddcoin team member hired called "Ricky0819".

On the 20th of January 2014 at 00:29:30 UTC, a Bitcointalk user fictitiously named "ReddCoin" announced a new cryptocurrency called Reddcoin, RDD. This official Reddcoin Bitcointalk thread was given the title "[ANN][IPO]Reddcoin [RDD] - the coin of the internet! Release on February 2th." As is evident from the title, some sort of IPO had been initiated besides the announcement. The very first response on this thread was made by user "Bfljosh" on the same day. He said:

> "sent 0,01 Btc."

This prior comment was most likely in reference to "Bfljosh" sending Bitcoin to the Initial Public Offering. Another user named "PinkPotatoes" said:

> "so a new version of doge?"

Several opening comments on the official Reddcoin Bitcointalk thread questioned the legitimacy of Reddcoin. Users questioned whether it was a scam coin, why another tip coin was necessary and the lack of initial communication between the founder and the initially engaged users from the cryptocurrency community.

It was clear from the opening discussion that an official website had already been created at www.reddcoin.com. A subreddit had already been created earlier on the 29th of April 2013. However, no Facebook or Twitter account existed at this time.

On the 22nd of January, the account of Bitcointalk user "ReddCoin" was flagged for being untrustworthy. He assured the community that Reddcoin is not a scam and trust would be built up throughout the initial launch, IPO and development stages. Also on this day, a decision was made to extend the availability of the IPO for another two weeks after the scheduled public launch of the coin. The main reason for this extension was to allow people to participate during development over the first two weeks after the 2nd of February. He was quoted as saying:

"We just noticed our account was flag for being untrusty and we feel we have to comment on this. We know some scam happen in the past here and you are right being prudent with your investment. Let me tell you why it won't happen this way. Hopefully, we can correct some misunderstanding. We have no reason to scam you. Why? Because you are getting coins in exchange for your investment. It's not like we had a reason not to give you those coins. It would only crash the value after everyone would get angry. The coin will be release on February 2th (it's already done and ready to go). We have decided to let our IPO run for two more weeks after we release the coin. This way, you will be able to judge the value of our work and decide at the last minute if you want to participate. It's a speculative investment. If you don't think our project will work, don't invest.

It could be a huge failure, we don't know for sure it will work. We already worked really hard on this project and we will kept working until we are done. We truly believe it's a great idea and it could become huge with social networks.

We know IPO are scammy, but unfortunately, it's our only way we can do it. We don't have enough money to invest in this project ourself, but we have some time and a lot of ideas. This is what we are offering you. IPO investor will receive their coins. We will invest all the IPO money in this project to develop the brand and our infrastructure.

We will do our best. Fell free to ask any questions you may have."

On the 26th of January at 21:47:12 UTC, changes to the block distribution schedule were announced. Firstly, the block halving rate was reduced from 525,600 to 500,000. This change alone would cause the block halving to occur approximately every 347 days. Also, it would create a total coin limit of 100,000,000,000 RDD. In addition to the former change, special block rewards for the first 30,000 blocks were implemented. This was to encourage, as well as gain the needed support from, miners during the first month. Bonus blocks would add an extra 8,946,710,000 RDD early on to the total circulation. The first block (block number 0) was the genesis block generated on the 21st of January with associated reward of 10,000 RDD. Below was the finalised block distribution table ready for the future public launch of the blockchain on the 2nd of February 2014:

Blocks	Reward	Total	Total Coin Circulation	Initial Block Date
1 (Genesis)	10,000	10,000	10,000.00	~21st January 2014
10 (IPCO)	545,000,000	5,450,000,000	5,450,010,000.00	~26th January 2014
9,989	300,000	2,996,700,000	8,446,710,000.00	~2nd February 2014
10,000	200,000	2,000,000,000	10,446,710,000.00	~9th February 2014
10,000	150,000	1,500,000,000	11,946,710,000.00	~16th February 2014
470,000	100,000	47,000,000,000	58,946,710,000.00	~23rd February 2014
500,000	50,000	25,000,000,000	83,946,710,000.00	~16th January 2015
500,000	25,000	12,500,000,000	96,446,710,000.00	~16th January 2016
500,000	12,500	6,250,000,000	102,696,710,000.00	~15th January 2017
500,000	6,250	3,125,000,000	105,821,710,000.00	~15th January 2018
500,000	3,125	1,562,500,000	107,384,210,000.00	~15th January 2019
500,000	0.762939453	381,469.7266	108,946,328,530.27	~12th January 2031
500,000	0.381469727	190,734.8633	108,946,519,265.14	~12th January 2032

This new block distribution table changed the total limit of coins to about 109 billion, or 108,946,710,000 RDD to be exact. The IPO percentage was also increased from the initial 3% to 5% (5,447,335,500 RDD). The block time was unchanged at 60 seconds and the difficulty re-target algorithm called the Kimoto Gravity Well was implemented. As can be seen, the supply would now grow at a faster rate.

Before the above announcement, block number one had already been pre-mined and timestamped to the blockchain at 21:31:34 UTC on the 26th of January.

Considering the IPO at this stage was only one phase, from the beginning to the 15th of February at 23:59 PST, Bitcointalk forum users were questioning it. One user called "templebar" on the 27th of January at 04:46:40 UTC said:

> "Interested. But where's the reward for early investors?
> May be you should consider two tier reward structure.
> One which closes on launch date and the other one two weeks after the launch for less risky people"

Other comments were made on this day too. The main agreement was that initial investors must have the best deal as they are taking the greatest risk. Later that day, "ReddCoin" responded to the above comment:

> "Early investor are the one taking part in the IPO. We only have 1 step of investor and registration close on february 15th.
> Thank you for your interest.
>
> Reddcoin"

However, again on the same day, "ReddCoin" proposed a new model for the IPO:

> "Hi everyone,
> Because we really care about this project and we want the best for Reddcoin, we are bringing something else to the table. Let us know what you think. We could split this IPO in 2 stages to reward really early investors.
> Stage 1 will close on february 1st at 11h59 PM PST before Reddcoin is released. Stage 2 stay the same and will close on february 15st at 11h59 PM PST.
> Stage 1 reward: 1.1 billion coins,
> Stage 2 reward: 4.35 billion coins.
> This is a 25% premium for early investors.
> On february 1st at 11h59 PM PST, we will take a snapshot of the database. All investors at the end of stage 1 will split 1.1 billion coins according to the amount of shares they own.
> All those investors will stay in for stage 2 where we will distribute the rest of the IPO, 4.35 billion coins according to the same formula.
> Every investor will still receive their coins during a period of 90 days after IPO close. This is done to protect the market. Let us know what you think.
> Reddcoin"

One reason why the IPO had been created was to raise capital (no reserve or required amount needed) to help towards coin development, the brand and continuation of built infrastructure. The founder and subsequent development team would otherwise find it difficult to fund future projects related to Reddcoin. It was said that the best will be done with the amount raised. On the 28th of January, there was debate over whether the term IPCO is more appropriate. IPO gave the wrong impression (creates confusion) as it suggested shares are offered at a fixed price. User "ReddCoin" made the following comment on the same day:

"Hi everyone,

I think I have to add some precisions to our project since some current investors are not happy with the way I do things.
This is not an actual IPO where we offer shares of our business at a fix price. Maybe we should have use another term, but we didn't. We are actually giving you a change to buy some Reddcoin before they are released at a price we believe will be good for you. It was clear from day 1. If owning those coins according to our terms is not ok with you, don't invest. We will change all our documentation to replace IPO with IPCO for Initial Public Coin Offering. We're sorry about the confusion we may have cause.
We have decided to stay anonymous with this project. This is the choice of most devs in the cryptocurrency world for obvious reasons. With all the story's on NSA and privacy breach everywhere, we prefer to stay anonymous as you probably all do. I don't have to reveal my identity when I sell stuff on ebay. It's the same here. If for you, this is a reason to not invest in our project, don't invest.
We already been transparent on the work we have done. No much is done beside Reddcoin, this IPO and our website.
Once again, if you have a problem with us being anonymous, don't invest. If you have a problem with our current strategy, don't invest.
Since we are clear and transparent about this, we will be offering refunds to investors who change their minds with this new information. You have until January 31st at 11h59 PST to request your refund. After that, there won't be any refund.
Contact us thru PM with your email address, investor ID and bitcoin address for refund.
Thank you

Reddcoin "

On the 29th of January, it was announced that a Reddcoin block explorer would be available on the day of the launch.

On the penultimate day of January at 07:00:52 UTC, user "ReddCoin" made an announcement regarding a new team member called "Ricky0819":

> "Hi everyone,
>
> I have great news! We've hired our first team member and he's our PR/Marketing Director - Ricky0819. Ricky0819 is a professional online marketing guy and has written up an awesome plan for the release of Reddcoin. He'll present his plan to you here in a bit. Looking forward to it!
>
> Reddcoin"

The response from user "Ricky0819" is presented on the adjacent page. On the 31st of January, he also made a quick marketing update:

> - We've hired 3 people for article/blog writing & social bookmarking.
> - Press release is almost complete and will be scheduled and ready to go tomorrow for the launch on Feb 2nd 😊
> - Adwords/Adcenter campaigns are being built and will begin running Feb 2nd as soon as coin is launched.
> - Facebook campaign will be built tomorrow to promote Fan Page
> - We are putting up a blog on reddcoin.com

At the end of the month, discussion on Bitcointalk occurred about whether the IPCO should last until the 2nd or the 15th of February. Is it really a risk to invest? Will early investors be rewarded more? Also, will an exchange exist before the 15th of February? "ReddCoin" was quoted as saying:

> "A word on the exchanges situation.
> We are fine with exchanges listing RDD. It's a free market and if people want to sell or buy Reddcoin we don't see any problem."

Six were actively working on the marketing of Reddcoin as the month closed.

Hey all!

Thanks for bringing me on board Redd 😵

So I came up with a bit of a marketing plan a little while ago and we're taking steps to cross some points off and

get the ball rolling on others. This should be an awesome launch with the push we intend to do! Here are the launch plans:

Multiple Press Release distribution/syndication through various PR Channels including PRWeb.com & PRLog.org

- Launch Date Press Release (Feb 2nd)

- End of IPCO Press Release (Feb 15th)

- Possible Press Release midway Feb 2nd & 5th

- Google AdWords, Bing/Yahoo AdCenter & other paid search campaigns – both search & display for continuous branding and visibility

- Hiring multiple blog & forum commenters for all crypto-related sites

- Hiring social bookmarker to link to all distributed content, website & blog/forum comments

- Expansion of website content – addition of a blog for news/updates/misc.

- Wikipedia article inclusion

- Guest blog posting on popular crypto blogs with high quality content

- Facebook Likes & CPM marketing campaigns to promote Fan Page and increase exposure

- Active Twitter updates & connecting with industry experts for expansion and follower building

Looking forward to getting this off the ground! I'll keep you all updated as things progress.
*** Also, if you'd like to help in anyway with any of these points - we'll gladly take all the help we can get! Feel free to email me at:
pr@reddcoin.com

Thanks!

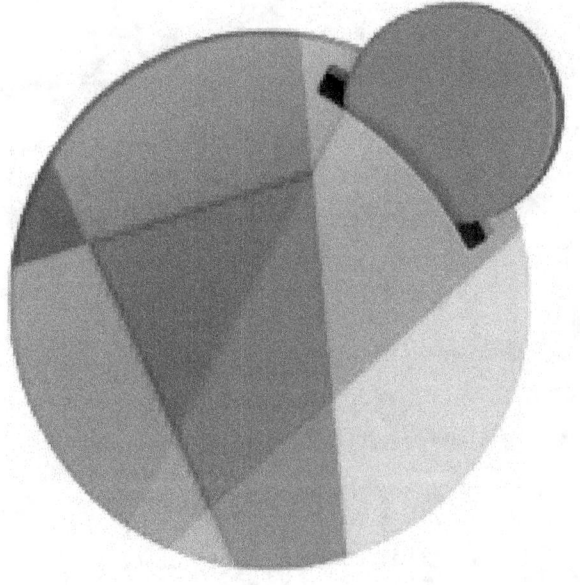

REDDCOIN IS PUBLICLY LAUNCHED

FEBRUARY 2014

I.   Reddcoin network protocol launched publicly.

II.   New Reddcoin logo chosen via 99Designs.

III.   Reddcoin began trading on seven exchanges.

IV.   Reddcoin added to the site www.coinmarketcap.com.

V.   Initial Public Coin Offering (IPCO) closed.

It was known from an announcement made in late January that the launch of the blockchain for community participation was scheduled to occur between 17:00-21:00 UTC on the 2nd of February. Miners were advised to pre-register with a Reddcoin supported mining pool as well as to make sure their mining equipment and software were ready. This ensured that they would be mining from the very first second. Some users of Bitcointalk described this as a surprise launch with no specific launch time. The reason why no definite launch time was chosen was so as to make sure nothing would crash due to users downloading the client at the same time. Even the mining pool operators did not know of the launch time. The plan was to release both the Windows wallet and the source code just before the launch.

On the 2nd of February at 06:55:47 UTC, "ReddCoin" announced a proposal to change the number of Reddcoin available in both stage one and stage two of the IPCO. He said:

> "Hi everyone,
>
> Sorry for being late to the discussion. I thought about this and here is what I think could be a good compromise. We really need your help in the next weeks and we need to work together so let me know what you all think.
>
> I'm ready to bring the reward for stage one to 2.2 billion. This is twice the current amount of 1.1 billion. This would left only 3.25 billion for the second stage and would give a huge advantage to stage one investors.
>
> Let me know what you think, we need to start working together on this if we all want to succeed.
>
> thank you for your support
>
> Reddcoin"

Later on, the first stage of the IPCO closed at 07:59 UTC. A total of about 55.32399750 BTC had been pledged from 245 investors. User "ReddCoin" announced the end of stage one at 08:10:34 UTC on the 2nd of February, about 11 minutes after the first stage closed.

After the initial Reddcoin had been pre-mined for the Initial Public Coin Offering, the blockchain was launched for miner participation at block number eleven. This block was generated at 15:53:57 UTC, about one hour before the scheduled time between 17:00 UTC and 21:00 UTC. This block generated a total of 300,000 RDD. However, the next block timestamped at 18:17:51 UTC after which the next blocks followed on quickly. Taking this into consideration, one could say that the launch did effectively begin within the planned time window except block eleven. Just before the launch, many Reddcoin related sites were understandably slow due to high traffic.

A few hours after the launch:

- The Windows wallet client v10 was released.

- A bounty of 0.1 BTC was offered for the first working Mac Wallet.

- Bitcointalk user "candidakefyr" announced the first block explorer for Reddcoin at http://cryptexplorer.com/chain/ReddCoin.

On the 3rd of February, Reddcoin began trading on three cryptocurrency exchanges. Bitcointalk user "def_ender" announced Freshmarket had added Reddcoin to their coin list ready for trading. At 07:53:13 UTC, he said:

> "Sup. I'm from freshmarket and we successfully added reddcoin to our coins list. It have to be mentioned that it's TEST MODE on redds, because dev still haven't answered us if it's ok to exchange this coin this early.
> So if redd DEV will insist on closing market - you will have to withdraw your REDDs and we will close market. Redds can be traded here:
> https://freshmarket.co.in/index.php?page=trade&market=136"

Bitcointalk forum user "coinmarket.io" at 11:15:13 UTC announced the RDD/BTC trading pair as live on CoinMarket.io. He said:

> "CoinMarket.io has opened the RDD/BTC market!
> https://www.coinmarket.io/market/RDDBTC
> 5 confirmations required for deposit, minimum amount for order 100 - might change to 1000 for all doge-style coins"

Later on the same day, user "def_ender" was quoted as saying:

> "I'm glad to say that freshmarket.co.in is reopened for REDD/LTC trades.
> We had conversation with devs and they told we can open at 18-00 CET, so we are. You'r welcome!
> https://freshmarket.co.in/index.php?page=trade&market=136"

The third exchange to add Reddcoin was Coin-Swap. This exchange closed down on the 22nd of March 2015. The other prior two have also since closed down.

On the 6th of February at 01:32:30 UTC, user "ReddCoin" announced the future release of version 1.1. The reason for this mandatory upgrade was due to a big mining pool upsetting the modified Kimoto Gravity Well settings initially implemented. It was working fine to begin with, but the Kimoto Gravity Well settings similar to Megacoin and Vertcoin would be used instead in v1.1. About two hours later, v1.1 was released. Users had until block number 6,000 to upgrade.

Two days later, Reddcoin began live trading on the exchange called CryptX.io. This exchange opened on the 8th of February and initially offered fifteen cryptocurrencies for active trading besides Reddcoin. It has since closed down.

On the following day, the block reward fell by one third:

Block #9,999 (Reward 300,000) Feb 9th 2014 at 12:34:58 PM UTC

Block #10,000 (Reward 200,000) Feb 9th 2014 at 12:35:15 PM UTC

On the 9th of February, Bitcointalk user "ricky0819" announced the coin logo design contest. A site called 99Designs was chosen as a means for designers to post their designs for the community to comment on or vote for. He said that the final coin logo would be chosen by the community. He was also quoted as saying:

"Regarding the idea behind the coin and the logo - it is meant to be integrated with social media so think of Facebook, Reddit, Twitter, Youtube colors (and other top social media sites).
Reddcoin is meant to be a global coin for users all over the world and easily understandable/recognizable.
We DO NOT have to have RED as the PRIMARY COLOR. That is NOT the point of Reddcoin. The letter R does NOT have to be in the logo (other than in the name "reddcoin").
In fact, most coins do this and it's boring and unoriginal (in my opinion!).
So with these conditions in mind, please rate each logo based on how well you think the designer captured the idea as well as how relevant the logo is to us, our cause and the general public because with the marketing we are going to be doing, we will be reaching millions."

A total of 525 coin logo designs were submitted by 141 designers. The bronze package CA$299 was used on the 99Designs website . Here are some of the most popular designs which were posted on the site:

#347 by Alexandark

#324 by NK1568

#323 by Daniel Exco

#319 by yoezer32

#283 by Xavier64

#159 by insanedio

#143 by berdoa

#346 by My Studio77

On the 14th of February at 01:33:22 UTC, user "ReddCoin" posted an update:

"Hi everyone,

It's been a couple of days since I gave an update so here it is! We are currently working a lot on Reddit to build our community. I think we have some great result to date. We are buying ads everywhere and they are clearly working great (around 2% clickthru on Reddit). We already have 465 Reddheads subscribe to our subreddit and it's growing every hour.

Our new logo should be ready soon, hopefully this week. It will be implement everywhere as soon as we receive the final version.

Ricky had some talk with one of our investor who owns a website creation business. He might work with us in the future, but I don't have any confirmation on this yet. We will start working on our new website as soon as we are done with the logo. Our main website will be our central hub where your single account will be linked to every social networks. No need for different account on each social networks.

Today, I finished testing my script to distribute the IPOC coins. I'm glad to inform you that it's working well and I won't have to send all those transactions one by one.

Let me know if you have any questions.

Thanks, Reddcoin"

On the following day, a winner of coin logo design contest on 99Designs was announced. Coin logo design number 347 designed by Alexandark won by a long shot. Design number 319 by yoezer32 was runner up. Both these coin logos can be seen more clearly on the previous page. However, logo #572 by Alexandra was ultimately chosen as shown on page 52. It replaced the coin logo on page 34.

On the 16th of February at 08:07:05 UTC, user "Reddcoin" announced the closure of the IPCO. The official time of closure was 23:59 PST on the 15th or 07:59 UTC on the 16th. In total from both stages, about 168.8 BTC (over 100K USD at the time) had been pledged from 386 investors. Each investor now knew their grand total of Reddcoin and would receive 1/90th of it each day for the next 90 days. Also, the Reddcoin developers had completed a script two days earlier that made it possible to send all daily IPCO payments in one go automatically instead of one by one. The table below displays the top ten investors besides their corresponding total entitlement of Reddcoin. On the same day at 16:37:56 UTC on Bitcointalk, user "ReddCoin" announced that the first 1.1111% (1/90th) had been sent. He requested users who had not received their daily payment to contact him as soon as possible. User "Xubu" said:

> "I can confirm that the first payment is in here.
> Thanks."

INVESTOR ID	AMOUNT (BTC)	% COINS	COINS STAGE 1	COINS STAGE 2	TOTAL COINS
497	9.28709067	7.77241	0	252,603,270	252,603,270
586	9.27000000	7.5399	0	245,046,830	245,046,830
499	9.00000000	7.12245	0	231,479,593	231,479,593
253	8.00000000	6.16645	213,838,626	200,409,534	414,248,160
233	7.80100000	5.86247	127,578,813	190,530,274	318,109,087
150	6.65500000	4.88049	1,998,604	158,615,948	160,614,552
213	5.92255000	4.24213	42,542,967	137,869,249	180,412,216
509	5.11050000	3.57809	0	116,287,768	116,287,768
588	5.10000000	3.49302	0	113,523,056	113,523,056
555	5.00000000	3.3524	0	108,953,044	108,953,044

Block #19,999 (Reward 200,000) Feb 16th 2014 at 02:34:42 PM UTC

Block #20,000 (Reward 150,000) Feb 16th 2014 at 02:34:46 PM UTC

A Windows wallet (version 1.1.1) was released on the 17th of February. It was not a mandatory upgrade because only cosmetic changes were made to the wallet client interface. In particular, the brand new Reddcoin logo was incorporated.

On the 20th of February, an exchange called Cryptorush introduced the trading pairs RDD/BTC, RDD/LTC and RDD/DOGE. Cryptorush went live on the 29th of January 2014 and has since closed down due to multiple hacking problems.

On the 23rd of February, the block reward generated by each block changed to 100,000 at which it would remain for about 327 days until the first block halving in January 2015 (On the 1st of May, v1.2.0.0 modified the first halving to occur on the 11th of May instead). All three of the block bonus phases were now complete.

Block #29,999 (Reward 150,000) Feb 23rd 2014 at 10:28:45 AM UTC

Block #30,000 (Reward 100,000) Feb 23rd 2014 at 10:30:13 AM UTC

Before the end of the month, two other cryptocurrency exchanges began to trade Reddcoin. These were Poloniex and Bittrex. Both these exchanges operate from the United States of America.

Poloniex added the trading pair REDD/BTC on their exchange on the 24th. This was about 36 days after the exchange was established on the 19th of January.

Bittrex is based in Seattle, Washington. It began operations on the 13th of February in beta testing mode during which time the trading pair RDD/BTC got listed on the 25th of February. Three days later, twelve cryptocurrencies and twenty one trading pairs were initially made available for trading besides Reddcoin as trading went live.

Members of the Reddcoin community were happy they were receiving their allocated 1.111% RDD of their investment each day. There were instances of investors not getting their daily share on time, but this was due to server problems. Nevertheless, payments were eventually received. Therefore, trust was build up between the development team and the rest of the community. One user called "zorkafdo" said:

> "Have been receiving the coins from IPCO everyday as promised.
> I initially thought that this was not going to happen.
> An honest admin, a great team and a great community = successful alt coin.
> Reddcoin in the right path."

Other events which occurred in the month of February were:

- An official Twitter Page was created shortly after the public launch.

- On the 2nd of February, the official Reddcoin Facebook Group was created.

- Coinmarketcap.com added Reddcoin to their list of cryptocurrencies on the 10th of February. It is a website on which the prices and trade volumes of a vast array of cryptocurrencies are continuously updated in real time.

- A bounty of 1 BTC was offered to anyone who was willing to create a fully functional Reddcoin Android wallet on the 20th of February.

- On the 25th of February, a Twitter Tipbot for Reddcoin went live. Since this time, it has been possible for users of Twitter to send each other RDD on this social media site.

CRYPTSY EXCHANGE AND REDDHEADS.COM
MARCH 2014

I.   Reddcoin Tipbot for Twitch.tv and Justin.tv launched.

II.   Reddcoin wallet client version 1.1.3 released.

III.   Reddcoin began trading on the Cryptsy cryptocurrency exchange.

IV.   Reddheads.com community blog created.

V.   Brand new design of the official website completed.

On the first day of March, an article was published titled "Top 100 digital currencies by social media presence" on the site www.crypt.la (http://crypt.la/2014/03/01/top-100-digital-currencies-by-social-media-presence/). The article listed many popular cryptocurrencies in order of their "social strength" on Facebook, Reddit and Twitter. In this instance, the most popular Twitter page or Facebook group for each coin was adopted to note how many people were following. Reddcoin was listed in fourth position with the following number of followers:

- Facebook — 3,581; Reddit — 1,311; Twitter — 31,200.

In total, this gave Reddcoin 36,092. Bitcoin unsurprisingly topped the table at 410,184 with Dogecoin second at 207,791. It is often said a cryptocurrency is as strong as the community that supports and participates in it.

One of the very first independent articles to be solely written about Reddcoin was posted online at the URL address http://www.business2community.com/tech-gadgets/reddcoin-social-media-meets-crypto-currency-0800202. It was published by Juergen Hoebarth on the 4th of March and titled "Reddcoin: When Social Media Meets Crypto Currency". His opening paragraph was:

> "The world's first crypto coin which is dedicated to tipping on social media. Have you ever wanted to give a little "thank you" to all the people helping you on twitter? Or the fans following and retweeting your tweets?"

He answered three questions:

- What is Reddcoin?

- How do I get started and get my first Reddcoins?

- How to tip people with Reddcoins on Twitter?

On the following day, user "ReddCoin" made an announcement concerning social media tipping:

> "I'd like to announce the arrival of two new Reddcoin Tipbots: one for Twitch.tv and one for Justin.tv, both of which have successfully finished closed beta testing."

Justin.tv is a generalised live streaming platform established in 2007 by Justin Kam and Emmett Shear. On the 6th of June 2011, a spin-off of Justin.tv was created called Twitch.tv. It is a live streaming platform specifically designed for video gaming. It was acquired by Amazon in September 2014 for about $970 million.

The Reddcoin community were encouraged to engage popular streamers on both sites about the benefits of donating RDD. One benefit of RDD cited was its inherent characteristic of being an irreversible method of payment. As a result, it eradicates the problem scam donations. This is very common with PayPal transactions which allow charge backs to occur. Another benefit emphasised at the time was that as streamers attract more viewers to their content and participate in donating RDD, their Reddcoin holdings should consequently increase in value over the long term.

Also on the 5th of March, users had difficulty synchronising their wallet clients (downloading the continuously updating blockchain). Many users complained that the client reached a particular block number after which no other blocks were downloaded. Also a very enormous difficulty number was evident. This led to some mining pools ceasing operations until a fix to the problem was found. "ReddCoin" stated a fix was on the way. At 15:11:06 UTC on the 6th of March, user "ReddCoin" said:

> "We had a fork on our last release.
> Please download v1.1.3 to fix the problem.
> After downloading and updating to v1.1.3, mining pools plus users were happy to get back onto the correct fork/chain of the blockchain."

Therefore, version 1.1.3 was ready for download and it was mandatory that users installed this latest upgrade. Users had to delete their existing downloaded blockchain and back-up their personal "wallet.dat" file (important file on which public/private keys are kept). It was highly recommended for users not to send this file to anyone they deemed untrustworthy. Also on this day, an exchange called Coined Up began trading Reddcoin (two trading pairs RDD/BTC and RDD/LTC).

On the 14th of March, Cryptsy began live trading of the pair RDD/BTC at https://www.cryptsy.com/markets/view/169. This exchange launched on the 20th of May 2013. It is based in Delray Beach, Florida, USA. It has become one of the most reputable cryptocurrency trading exchanges. It is still active today.

Six days later, another exchange called AGX.io initiated live trading of the pair RDD/BTC on their platform. The exchange was announced in early February 2014 on the Bitcointalk forum and registrations to sign up to it were possible from the 27th of February. It went live on the 15th of March. It closed its doors the same year.

On the 21st of March, an article was published titled "Reddcoin: The Rising Social Currency" at https://www.cryptocoinsnews.com written by Drew Cordell. He interviewed the lead developer of Reddcoin called Laudney. A transcript of this interview can be found in the appendix of this book.

On the 21st of March, the first article on www.reddheads.com was published. It was written by blogger Melissa. Reddheads.com is a community blog for Reddcoin enthusiasts to provide commentary about Reddcoin news, events and general information. Her last paragraph in the article was:

> "People everyday of their lives use email, they probably have no idea how it works under the covers, but they use it because it's simple, free, easy, and allows them to send messages anywhere in the world for free. It's the same thing with Bitcoin, send money anywhere in the world for free."

After about five weeks of trading, the exchange called Cryptorush was experiencing problems with its trading platform. Laudney, the lead developer of Reddcoin, made an annoucement on the official blog regarding the issue. He advised members of the Reddcoin community, Reddheads, to withdraw their holdings from the exchange, especially after the exchange had lost the majority of Blackcoins (another cryptocurrency). This announcement was made on the 26th of March 2014:

> "Fellow Reddheads
>
> I normally don't make announcement like this but after very much research on my side I've concluded that the people running the
>
> exchange are extremely incompetent and according to this insider's latest shocking revelation the exchange is insolvent for some time.
>
> Then yesterday we witnessed the Blackcoin fiasco.
>
> I hope I'm wrong but you have been warned.
>
> Regards
>
> Laudney"

By the end of the month, a total of eleven cryptocurrency exchanges had already added Reddcoin to their exchanges for active trading. Only three of these exchanges still exist at the time of publication of this book. These are Bittrex, Cryptsy and Poloniex.

On the last day of March, the official website had been successfully redesigned. Laudney gave thanks for all the feedback from the community, the work from BTCillionaire and the support from the rest of the development team. It was BTCillionaire who announced the redesign at http://new.reddcoin.com on the 29th of March. He said the design was inspired by the recent PayPal website at the time. With a more professional feel, he was confident that it would help set Reddcoin apart from all the other cryptocurrencies and also emphasise the social aspect of Reddcoin. The fourth response to the announcement post was from Reddit user "reddki" on the same day at 12:15:52 UTC. He said:

> "This is more than an improvement. Absolutely amazing.
> Congratulations on this achievement, mate."

Other events which occurred in the month of March were:

- On the 8th of March, pmtocoins.com became the ninth exchange to initiate Reddcoin trading.

- The official Reddcoin Android wallet was released on Google Play on the 12th of March. Members of the community were encouraged to install it and inform the developer if any bugs were discovered.

- An altcoinpress.com article was written by Greg Matthews titled "Reddcoin: It's All About the Community Dummy" on the 21st of March. It was published at 23:09 ET.

According to the site www.cryptocoincharts.info, the Bitcoin Satoshi price of Reddcoin was trading in the range 4-6 on the last day of March. The following table displays the values from two exchanges:

	Price	Low	Open	Close	High	Volume (BTC)
Cryptsy	4.5	4	4	4	5	4.25952
Coined Up	5.5	4	5	6	6	0.0362397

PROOF OF STAKE VELOCITY ANNOUNCMENT
APRIL 2014

I.   Reddcoin wallet client version 1.1.3.2 released.

II.   Reddcoin Broadcast went live.

III.   Reddcoin began to trade on Prelude by Moolah.

IV.   Reddcoin wallet client version 1.1.3.3 released.

V.   New Proof of Stake Velocity (PoSV) timestamping algorithm announced.

At the beginning of April, the Reddcoin community had achieved over 10,000 subscribers on its official Reddcoin subreddit. This was a lot more than other cryptocurrencies had attained within a similar timeframe since their respective launch dates.

Laudney, the lead developer of Reddcoin, reminded members of the community of a current method on which discussion about the coin can occur. An IRC channel, #reddcoin on irc.freenode.net, has been available on which answers to questions can be sought after in minutes if not seconds.

In the first week of the month, there were many events to celebrate after the release of the new official website. Some of these included the launch of the ReddAPI, the Reddcoin Tipping Platform Chrome extension, Firefox extension and multiple ongoing subreddit tipping campaigns.

On the 6th of April, Reddcoin began to trade on the exchange called Swisscex. The exchange does not exist now. It went active on the 1st of February 2014 and is based in Switzerland. In early February 2014, a total of 100 different trading pairs for just over 40 cryptocurrencies were active. It was operated by Swiss individuals who established it in January 2014.

A mandatory upgrade to the Reddcoin wallet (v1.1.3.2) was released on the 9th of April in order to protect the code from the Heartbleed Security Bug. Reddcoin team member Reddki described what the Heartbleed Security Bug is:

"When the bug is exploited the attacker can retrieve memory (up to 64kb) from the remote system. This memory may contain usernames, passwords, keys or other useful information that enables bigger attacks. An attacker may for example be able to retrieve the keys and secrets used to encrypt traffic and then intercept and read the communications of all other users of that service. There are all kinds of variations that might be possible based on the ability to read this memory. 64kb may not seem like a great deal of data, but of course the attacker can connect repeatedly and progressively collect more information."

One day later, user "ReddCoin" on Bitcointalk at 00:14:37 UTC said:

"Hi everyone,
We have release our new wallet 1.1.3.2 which uses the latest OpenSSL 1.0.1g with fix for Heartbleed security bug. Update is mandatory.
thanks
Reddcoin"

Three days later, a website called Reddcoin Broadcast went live (https://broadcast.reddcoin.com/). It is a social broadcast platform that helps spread a message or idea. It works by sharing the idea with one's individual social media contacts and encouraging people who receive the broadcast to share it with their contacts. One can also encourage fellow forum members to spread the message through their social media connections too. On the same day, user "ReddCoin" in reference to the new website said:

"AMPLIES YOUR MESSAGE WITH THE SUPPORT OF THE CROWD"

A total of twelve Reddcoin community videos were released during the month. These videos are still accessible on YouTube at the time of publication of this book. Members of the community were being creative and supportive of Reddcoin:

Reddcoin Promo
9th of April

Reddcoin: The Social Currency
10th of April

(Reddcoin Tip and Upvote Reminder #1 - Puppet Edition) - 10th of April

(Reddcoin Tip and Upvote Reminder #2 - The Puppet Rap) - 14th of April

Reddcoin Tip & Upvote Reminder #3 - The Preacher - 16th of April

Reddcoin Tip and Upvote Reminder #4 - The Frenchman) - 18th of April

Reddcoin Tip and Upvote Reminder #5 - An Easter Message - 19th of April

Reddcoin Is Happy (feat. Ana Cristina and Pharrel Williams) - 23rd April

A Thank You to the Reddcoin Community #1) - 24th April

One Million Reddcoin Bet: A Slap to the Face) 25th of April

I Tried to Buy an Apple for 5 Reddcoins #1 - 28th of April

Reddcoin Did you know? #1: Reddcoin, The Revolutionary - 30th of April

On the 20th of April, the thirteenth cryptocurrency exchange began to trade Reddcoin. AllCrypt was announced on the 29th of January 2014. From the 4th of February, users were able to register and then vote for their favourite coins to be added on the platform. The exchange opened for active trading on the 28th of February 2014. It is no longer active.

Two days later, Reddcoin began to trade live on Prelude.io by Moolah against BTC and USD. It was the first exchange to implement direct trading between Reddcoin and the US Dollar. In late 2014, the exchange closed down due to maintenance issues and continued hack attacks. On the 23rd of April, Reddki on Reddheads.com was quoted as saying:

> "No longer will Reddheads be required to purchase Bitcoin with fiat and then convert Bitcoin to Reddcoin – it's now a direct purchase.
> This is amazing news for Reddcoin and I have no doubt the Reddcoin community will support Moolah's Prelude.io as a sign of appreciation. Moolah has been a huge driving force behind Dogecoin and we're glad he's now on board with RDD.
> "How do I buy Reddcoin?" It's a piece of cake."

PRELUDE
BY MOOLAH

One day later, a maintenance wallet upgrade (v1.1.3.3) was made available for download and installation via github. It was not mandatory, but was highly recommended since it would improve security and speed of the client. Reddki said:

> "Reddcoin blockchain checkpoints have been updated in order to assist faster syncing speeds and to provide protection against future forks. Please update as soon as possible."

On the 29th of April at 07:24:03 UTC, an official announcement was made by Laudney regarding a future change of the timestamping algorithm. His announcement was as follows:

"Dear fellow Reddheads:

After long period of research and development, the Reddcoin core team decides the time is now right to announce the biggest milestone in Reddcoin history to date.

We have designed a new algorithm called Proof-of-Stake-Velocity (PoSV) to replace the current Proof-of-Work (PoW).

PoSV builds on the strength of Proof-of-Stake (PoS) but introduces crucial features to address the flaws of both PoW and PoS.

PoSV is *specifically* designed to help Reddcoin grow as *the digital social currency*.

We urge you all to read both papers carefully. We've taken great efforts to document *why* and *how* we designed PoSV to solve *what* problems. We've also spelt out the *vision* for Reddcoin and its *unique position* in the competitive landscape of cryptocurrencies.

The release of wallet 1.2.0.0 will happen tomorrow.

Please post *thoughtful* comments and questions below. Flaming will be removed immediately.

Regards, Reddcoin core team"

The full design white paper on proof of stake velocity titled "Proof of Stake Velocity: Building the Social Currency of the Digital Age" is in the appendix.

According to www.bitinfocharts.com, the price of one Reddcoin unit of account was roughly $0.000038 (26,316 RDD per $1) on the 30th of April. On the most popular exchange called Cryptsy, the Bitcoin Satoshi value of one RDD was 8 Satoshi.

NEW BLOCK DISTRIBUTION SCHEDULE
AND IPCO DISTRIBUTION COMPLETE
MAY 2014

I.   Reddcoin wallet client version 1.2.0.0 released.

II.   First block halving from 100,000 RDD to 50,000 RDD occurred.

III.   Cryptsy 51% attack executed.

IV.   Reddcoin IPCO distribution complete.

V.   Further Reddcoin community videos published.

As promised at the end of April, an upgrade to the Reddcoin wallet client was punctually released. It introduced a more accurate estimation of the network hashrate and a new block distribution schedule. On the 1st of May, user "ReddCoin" announced this upgrade on Bitcointalk at 14:43:10 UTC. He said:

> "Hi everyone,
>
> Wallet 1.2.0.0 is now officially released.
> Absolutely everybody needs to upgrade ASAP!
> http://www.reddit.com/r/reddCoin/comments/24efyz/
> mandatory_upgrade_asap_wallet_1200_is_now_released/
> Block reward going down to 50k on may 10th/11th!
>
> thanks
> Reddcoin"

Laudney emphasised that users needed to upgrade to this latest version as soon as possible, otherwise they would find themselves on a wrong fork of the blockchain. They would also potentially lose their coins after the first block halving. This halving was scheduled to happen on the evening 10th May in the US and early morning 11th May in Europe at block number 140,000. After this date, the block reward would halve approximately every 35 days (34.72 days to be more exact) as can be seen in the table below. A new total cap of 27,946,710,000 RDD had now been set. Taking into account the old cap of about 108,946,710,000 RDD, 81,000,000,000 less coins would be generated (a 74.35% decrease in projected supply).

Blocks	Reward	Total	Total Coin Circulation	Initial Block Date
1	10,000	10,000	10,000	~21st January 2014
10 (IPCO)	545,000,000	5,450,000,000	5,450,010,000	~26th January 2014
9,989	300,000	2,996,700,000	8,446,710,000	~2nd February 2014
10,000	200,000	2,000,000,000	10,446,710,000	~9th February 2014
10,000	150,000	1,500,000,000	11,946,710,000	~16th February 2014
110,000	100,000	11,000,000,000	22,946,710,000	~23rd February 2014
50,000	50,000	2,500,000,000	25,446,710,000	~11th May 2014
50,000	25,000	1,125,000,000	26,696,710,000	~14th June 2014
50,000	12,500	625,000,000	27,321,710,000	~19th July 2014

Until implementation of PoSV, the block reward will continue to halve every 50,000 blocks

Laudney also made a further announcement besides the above wallet release regarding a future upgrade. He said:

"In coming months we'll release alpha and beta release of wallet 1.3.0.0 that implements PoSV and will invite volunteers to try out the new minting process on Reddcoin testnet. Stay tuned."

In order to celebrate the upcoming block halving, the community announced an event called "#Tip Reddcoin Week" to begin on the 4th of May and finish on the 10th of May. A poster was designed for the occasion, which is visible on page 64.

On the 9th of May, the exchanges CryptX, Poloniex, Bittrex, Coined Up, Cryptsy, Swisscex, AllCrypt and Prelude all confirmed that they had upgraded to the latest wallet version 1.2.0.0. They were all ready for the block halving.

Block #139,999 (Reward 100,000) May 11th 2014 at 02:42:12 AM UTC

Block #140,000 (Reward 50,000) May 11th 2014 at 02:45:13 AM UTC

On the 11th of May, the block reward halved (see above).

In the middle of May, an individual or group launched a double spending attack on the Cryptsy exchange through the Reddcoin network protocol. He had accumulated over fifty percent of the overall hash power so was able to generate a private blockchain longer than the public chain. He gained Bitcoin from this practice after six confirmations (six minutes). The Reddcoin developers noticed anomalies in the network so notified Cryptsy to increase the number of confirmations to sixty. Consequently, this made future attacks more costly and slower to execute. One user rented 1.5 Gh/s of hashing power in order to deprive the attacker of his majority holding of hashing power.

At a later date, Cryptsy set the number of confirmations for deposits and withdrawals at 999. This was done to further secure the network against 51% attacks. The developers were looking forward to the change of timestamping algorithm to PoSV because it would render these attacks useless after its future implementation.

On the 16th of May, the distribution of Reddcoin to the initial IPCO investors ended. Ninety days had passed since the start of the disbursement of RDD. Funds (BTC) raised from this had helped to secure Reddcoin by adding extra hashing power. Reddki on Reddheads.com was quoted as saying:

"The 90 day Reddcoin IPO distribution for investors is now complete. Due to the number of coins being distributed daily, this essentially equates to another halving, which is great new for those who invested both before and after the IPO. The Reddcoin IPO has been the most successful cryptocurrency investor scheme to date. Funds raised by the Reddcoin development team have been used to not only develop Reddcoin, but most importantly, to secure the Reddcoin network."

Again, a total of twelve further Reddcoin community videos were released during the month of May. These videos on YouTube show the worldwide appeal of Reddcoin:

On the 22nd of May, a cryptocurrency exchange called Coin Next began active trading of Reddcoin. It was the only exchange to add Reddcoin in May.

On the 28th of May, Reddki announced the second "#Tip Reddcoin Week" scheduled to occur from the 1st of June to the 8th of June. The preceding "#Tip Reddcoin Week" was a success. It was another opportunity for the community to tip friends and admire online social content. A poster had already been prepared:

Other events which occurred in the month of May were:

- On the 6th of May, version 1.04 of the Reddcoin Android Wallet was released on Google Play.

- The "Reddcoin Mintpal Exchange Campaign" to help get Reddcoin listed on the exchange Mintpal began on the 19th of May.

- Annette Lawless, an anchor-reporter for KAKE News, Wichita, Kansas at the time, tweeted about RDD to 14,800 of her followers on the 24th of May.

- A total of three Q&A sessions were held between the developers and community members.

ANNOUNCEMENT OF NEXT GENERATION
SOCIAL WALLET
JUNE 2014

I.   A video on YouTube called "How do I buy Reddcoin?" was published

II.   Proof of Stake Velocity algorithm ready for internal testing.

III.   Reddcoin wallet client version 1.2.1.0 released.

IV.   Next generation social wallet announced.

V.   First proof of stake velocity block found on testnet.

On the second day of June, a video was published on YouTube titled "[Reddcoin Official] How do I buy Reddcoin?". Its main objective is to help describe the Reddcoin purchasing process through a colourful animation. It recommends the purchase of Bitcoin initially via one of four exchanges:

- Coinbase.com   -based in the United States of America.

- Bitstamp.net   -based in Europe.

- Vaultofsatoshi.com -based in Canada.

- Coinjar.io   -based in Australia.

Following on, the video recommends Cryptsy and Poloniex as two trusted exchanges on which Reddcoin can be bought. At the end of the video, viewers are made aware of the availability of the Reddcoin wallet on the official website.

Two days later, user "ReddCoin" was quoted as saying:

> "PoSV is ready for testing.
>
> http://www.reddit.com/r/reddCoin/comments/278fux/
> a_few_more_days_before_internal_private_testing/"

On the 8th of June, lead developer Laudney announced on the Reddcoin subreddit at 00:37:10 UTC that the first phase, one of three, of internal proof of stake velocity (PoSV) testing was complete. The developers were happy to notify the community that PoSV development was ahead of schedule.

Two days later, a new upgrade of the qt/daemon wallet (v1.2.1.0) was made available for download. It was not mandatory, but it was highly recommended users upgraded due to some new features including most recent security fixes, faster blockchain syncing speeds and a new splash (interface image) for the wallet.

On the 14th of June at 18:21:19 UTC, Laudney announced the next generation social wallet for Reddcoin on the official subreddit. For a few months, user "u/hoppipoppipolla" had been working on this innovative wallet. It incorporates live chat, news feed and the usual facility to hold Reddcoin. Other features were also being planned for inclusion. The social wallet would be set apart from the traditional qt wallet in the sense of having a more vibrant user interface. It would be available for Windows, Mac and Linux operating systems ready for release in the coming weeks after beta testing.

Shortly after the above announcement, the block reward halved at block number 190,000. A total of 25,446,710,000 RDD had now been generated via Scrypt proof of work mining. Consequently, the percentage of coins mined was about 90% now.

Block #189,999 (Reward 50,000) June 14th 2014 at 07:20:05 PM UTC

Block #190,000 (Reward 25,000) June 14th 2014 at 07:20:47 PM UTC

On the 18th of June, internal testing of PoSV on testnet entered its final phase. At the end of the announcement by Laudney, he said:

> "After internal testing finishes, I'll start invitation-only beta testing followed by public beta. Stay tuned."

Six days later, Laudney asked technically minded members of the community to volunteer towards the testing of PoSV. In particular, he wanted people to mint/stake PoSV blocks on testnet.

Other events which occurred in the month of June were:

- One community video was published on YouTube on the 3rd of June. It is titled "The Men In Blue Officially Support Reddcoin".

- No exchanges began to trade Reddcoin in June.

- The first PoSV block was found on testnet on the 23rd of June (see below).

- On the 30th of June, Reddcoin was positioned at number five on the Mintpal voting list of potential coin additions to this exchange.

```
2014-06-23 00:40:19 CreateCoinStake : added kernel type=1
2014-06-23 00:40:19 CBlock::SignBlock : coinstake created
2014-06-23 00:40:19 GetStakeModifierSelectionInterval : 2087
2014-06-23 00:40:19 GetKernelStakeModifier : nStakeModifierHeight=2089
2014-06-23 00:40:19 GetKernelStakeModifier : nStakeModifierHeight=2091
2014-06-23 00:40:19 GetKernelStakeModifier : nStakeModifierHeight=2093
2014-06-23 00:40:19 GetKernelStakeModifier : nStakeModifierHeight=2095
2014-06-23 00:40:19 GetKernelStakeModifier : nStakeModifierHeight=2097
2014-06-23 00:40:19 CheckStakeKernelHash() : using modifier 0x00000000000000
 for block from height=2085 timestamp=2014-06-22 17:39:14 UTC
2014-06-23 00:40:19 CheckStakeKernelHash() : check modifier=0x00000000000000
xPrev=0 nPrevout=0 nTimeTx=1403484020 hashProof=20fcfc690b0496df30c5482c920f
2014-06-23 00:40:19 CheckStake() : new proof-of-stake-velocity block found
 hash: b1b98ad71e6eea1dc88bc80b316d3f715193a2fbfd06eac47a11d76b59cd90b9
 proofhash: 20fcfc690b0496df30c5482c920fd9d0ef7d3e3a43a45e32a21e25d146524a1
 target: 6ce8291f56000000000000000000000000000000000000000000000000000000
2014-06-23 00:40:19 CBlock(hash=b1b98ad71e6eea1dc88bc80b316d3f715193a2fbfd06
aeb2457836bb1b57ffc6e295993bdd848cfb7aeaebb0d410fd8f2386c901e0564ed07f88e363
1e00000000, PoW=6e55d529c126dc1b1c6cadc3e2fbdf3a0cd83f01c442aa7536a27d13e498
59296efc7fb5b16b835724eb2a38b7844e5a2600, hashMerkleRoot=c338df7786f460b21a5
e=1403484020, nBits=1e0fffff, nNonce=0, vtx=2, vchBlockSig=3045022035e08766s
```

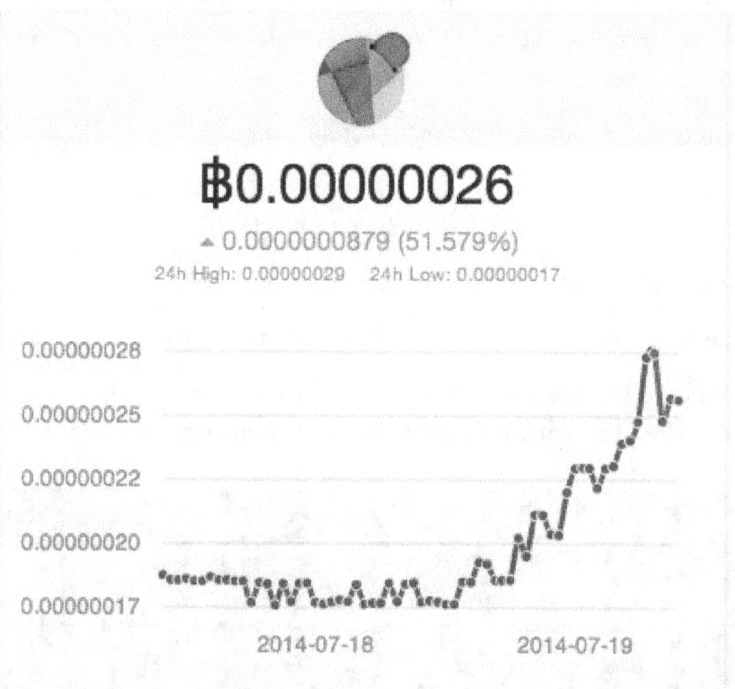

MARKET CAPITALISATION SURGE
AND VERSION 1.3.0.0 WALLET RELEASED

JULY 2014

I.   Proof of stake velocity mass minting/staking executed on testnet.

II.   Final block reward halving reached.

III.   Reddcoin wallet client version 1.3.0.0 released.

IV.   All time high market capitalisation of Reddcoin in 2014 reached.

V.   Reddcoin began trading on the exchanges called Mintpal and AllCoin.

Throughout the first several days of July, the main subject of discussion concerned further testing of PoSV. On the 2nd of July, Laudney announced that the testing of mass minting/staking would occur very soon. Two days later, he notified the community on Reddit of future developments. At 07:31:50 UTC, he said:

> "I'm going to release the public alpha version of PoSV daemon and QT wallet in coming days, probably as early as this weekend. In order to start minting straight away when you get hold of the wallet, you need to mine and age some coins on testnet now."

On the 6th of July, the public alpha release of the PoSV wallet client was made available on github. Laudney emphasised that testing should be left to the most "tech-savvy" of Reddcoin community members.

On the following day, 2,200 PoSV blocks had already been successfully minted via means of the alpha client on testnet. Nevertheless, Laudney asked for extra help from the community. He politely requested further volunteers to download the alpha software and then participate in minting PoSV blocks. This would then ensure a more thorough testing of the new code and a sooner launch date of PoSV.

Another discussion at the beginning of the month was about getting Reddcoin added to Mintpal, a new cryptocurrency exchange. In the previous month, members of the Reddcoin community were encouraged to visit the official voting page of future cryptocurrency additions and vote for Reddcoin. On the 1st of July, Reddcoin had reached number four in the voting list of all coins fighting to get listed. On the same day, Bitcointalk forum user "nightengale" at 11:29:32 UTC said:

> "Now number 4 on MintPal, 3 is within striking distance.
> Awesome community."

In order to build upon this position in the pursuit for number one position, a campaign was initiated by Reddcoin subreddit user "YooneekYoosahNeahm" at 15:38:31 UTC on the 1st of July titled "Mintpal Vote Drive Thread July 1-2". He said:

> "Ive decided to extend the competition to when we are added to mintpal.
> I humbly request someone maintain a count of everyone's votes.
> you will be rewarded for your effort.
>
> If you vote on Minpal post your vote number here and be tipped 5000 RDD.
> The top 5 voters will win 500k RDD. The next 5 200k RDD.
> Everyone else over 10 votes 15k RDD. My tipjar could also use some love.
> I'm just going to pay it forward. SHOUTOUT TO JimmyTheJ for the generous
> donation towards the drive!"

Further campaigns to encourage voting for Reddcoin on Mintpal were initiated on the 3rd, 4th and 9th of July. The drive to get Reddcoin on Mintpal had hastened.

Beginning on the 6th of July, a large upswing in price in terms of BTC Satoshi (1 BTC Satoshi = 0.00000001 BTC) occurred. The following table displays the BTC Satoshi value of Reddcoin on Cryptsy according to values obtained from the website called www.cryptocoincharts.info:

	Price	Low	Open	Close	High	Volume (BTC)
1st July	6.5	5	6	7	8	19.1123
2nd July	7	6	7	7	8	15.1419
3rd July	7.5	7	7	8	8	4.89807
4th July	7	7	8	7	8	7.64225
5th July	7	7	7	7	8	12.0445
6th July	8.5	7	7	10	10	40.9968
7th July	10	8	10	10	12	64.4594

As can be seen from the preceding table, there was a substantial increase in the daily trading volume on the last two days. This was the first time the price had gone above the ten Satoshi threshold, since it peaked at 14 Satoshi on Coined Up back in March. In doing so, the USD price of one unit of RDD account had surpassed $0.00005 (20,000 RDD = 1 USD).

Two further YouTube videos were published on the 5th and 10th of July:

Let's Go—A Reddcoin Rap

5th of July 2014

You're Invited to the Reddcoin Block Halving Party!

10th of July 2014

On the 10th of July, Reddcoin reached number one position on Mintpal's voting list of potential coin additions to their exchange.

From the 12th to the 18th of July, the price of one RDD unit of account had increased from 10 to 28 BTC Satoshi (an increase of 180%).

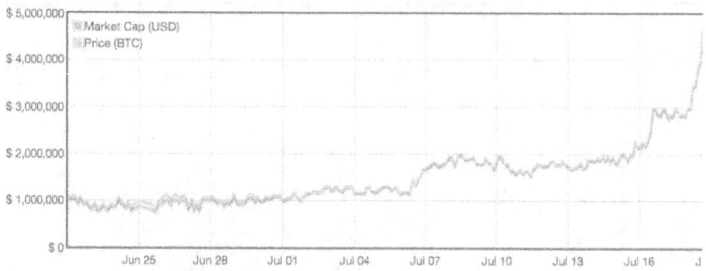

One day before the reward halved, Reddcoin began live trading on Mintpal. Mintpal launched on the 5th of February 2014 and registered a first day volume of just over 60 BTC. On their official Twitter page, Mintpal announced the addition:

> "A delayed congratulations to Reddcoin (RDD) for winning our voting on Monday.
> We have now put the market live.
> https://www.mintpal.com/market/RDD/BTC [1/2]"

Straight after its addition to this exchange, the number of confirmations in order to deposit and withdraw Reddcoin was set to 2,000. This was a security measure enforced to protect Reddcoin against the possibility of future 51% attacks. It would help to ensure a smooth migration to proof of stake velocity in the coming weeks.

In the early hours of the 19th of July, the block reward halved. At the time, it was described as the last halving before PoSV implementation. This implied that the network protocol would migrate to PoSV within the next 35 days.

Block #239,999 (Reward 25,000) July 19th 2014 at 05:39:56 AM UTC

Block #240,000 (Reward 12,500) July 19th 2014 at 05:41:23 AM UTC

On the 23rd of July at 20:52:05 UTC, Laudney created a new post on the Reddcoin subreddit to notify the community that the new official mandatory wallet upgrade (v1.3.0.0) was available. He was quoted as saying:

> "Dear fellow Reddheads:
> PoSV is now officially released. You can download the PoSV wallet v1.3.0.0 for Windows/ Linux/Mac at this link. PoSV will start at block 260800 which is expected to be *minted* around 7pm UTC, 2nd August 2014. (Who will be the lucky one?) The total amount of RDD mined in PoW phase will be just a tad shy of 27 billion, which is about 500m less than we originally estimated.
>
> ...(technical material)...
>
> Finally, a huge thank you to all who have helped us test PoSV. It's your efforts and contribution that make this release possible.
>
> Regards, laudney"

In order to make sure this message was not missed by anyone, it was also posted on Bitcointalk at 21:47:17 UTC. This supported the fact that community discussion had become more predominant on Reddit than on Bitcointalk. User "allcoinminer" was the first one to respond to the above announcement on Bitcointalk. He said:

> "Great News finally came. On to PoSV now!
> PoSV Countdown http://www.reddcoinhub.com/posvcountdown/"

The next reply was by user "dandruff1138". He said:

> "Wow I didn't expect this until August!"

As a consequence of the upcoming end of proof of work mining at block number 260,799, only an extra 260 million Reddcoin would be generated from the 19th of July up to the 2nd of August. As estimated above by Laudney , the total number of Reddcoin mined via PoW would be 26,956,710,000 exactly.

Following on from the initial upsurge in price at the end of the first week of July, the price continued to rise until a peak was reached for the year 2014 . On the 26th of July, the BTC Satoshi value of one RDD unit of account equalled the value of one DOGE unit of account. User "dandruff1138" on Bitcointalk at 15:03:51 UTC said:

> "Currently tied with DOGE at 35, will RDD overtake DOGE?"

At the peak, a high of 41 BTC Satoshi was recorded on Cryptsy besides a corresponding total daily trading volume of about 939 BTC on the 27th of July. On five exchanges on that date, the trading figures of RDD/BTC markets according to www.cryptocoincharts.info were:

	Price (BTC Satoshi)	Low (BTC Satoshi)	Open (BTC Satoshi)	Close (BTC Satoshi)	High (BTC Satoshi)	Volume (BTC Satoshi)
Cryptsy	37.5	28	40	35	41	938.555
Bittrex	33.5	30	36	31	40	25.7193
Mintpal	36	32	39	33	41	15.878
Swisscex	36	33	35	37	97	13.1985
Bleutrade	38.5	32	32	45	45	0.001456

In terms of a USD price, the site www.bitinfocharts.com recorded a value of approximately $0.0002 for one RDD unit of account ($1 = 5,000 RDD) at the peak.

According to www.coinmarketcap.com, a total market capitalisation of about $6,373,318 was recorded at the peak. It is safe to say that the market capitalisation surpassed $6 million, regardless of which method is used to calculate it.

On the 29th of July, Reddcoin began live trading on AllCoin as the trading pair RDD/BTC. A post on the official Reddcoin Bitcointalk thread was submitted to notify the community. User "btc-mark" on this thread said:

"Hi,
we've added RDD/BTC market, happy trading.

https://www.allcoin.com/trade/RDD_BTC"

On the same day, it was confirmed that all active exchanges had upgraded to the latest version of the client (v1.3.0.0).

Other events in the month of July were:

- A new unmoderated Reddcoin subreddit called "ReddPlayground" was created (.../r/reddplayground/) on the 6th of July. On here, a conservation about price and rumours could occur instead of such discussions saturating the main Reddcoin Subreddit (.../r/reddcion/). As a result, the main subreddit would look more professional and easier to navigate through.

- Reddcoin began active trading on the exchange called Bleutrade on the 17th of July.

- Cryptsy initiated the trading pair RDD/USD to their trading platform on the 20th of July.

- On the 27th of July, a site went live on which one could easily buy Reddcoin directly by using PayPal (www.wesellredd.com). It is currently called WeSellCrypto. It offers DOGE, RDD, LTC, DASH and XPY.

- On the 28th of July, the official Reddcoin video was almost complete.

THE LAUNCH OF PROOF OF STAKE VELOCITY

AUGUST 2014

I.   Reddcoin Roadmap published.

II.   Proof of Stake Velocity began at block number 260,800.

III. Next-Generation Reddcoin Social Wallet (v1.0.0) released.

IV.   Latest "#Tip Reddcoin Week" occurred to celebrate PoSV.

V.   Reddcoin Wikipedia introduced to the community.

Before the inevitable switch of timestamping algorithm to PoSV, the development team published a graphic called the Reddcoin Roadmap. It displays the future stages of development scheduled for the rest for the year 2014 and beyond. A copy of it can be found in the appendix of this book.

In anticipation of block number 260,800 (the first PoSV block), user "dandruff1138" at 12:28:37 UTC on the 2nd of August 2014 said:

> "6 hours until PoSV begins. 😊 Congratulations everyone!"

In order for community members to keep track of the time until block number 260,800, a countdown timer had been developed and was accessible at the website http://www.reddcoinhub.com/posvcountdown.

Block #260,799 (Reward 12,500) August 2nd 2014 at 05:19:58 PM UTC

Block #260,800 (Reward PoSV) August 2nd 2014 at 05:20:34 PM UTC

On the official Reddcoin Bitcointalk thread, user "ReddCoin" notified the community of the timestamping algorithm switch and the launch of the new official Reddcoin video titled "What is Reddcoin?". On the 2nd of August at 18:57:40 UTC, he said:

PoSV is live and our Official video is out!

https://www.youtube.com/watch?v=KlYJ0sNVVpg

About four hours after the first PoSV block, a mandatory wallet upgrade was made available. Laudney announced it on the Reddcoin subreddit at 21:17:24 UTC:

"Dear fellow Reddheads:

Mandatory upgrade to wallet v1.3.1.0

Thanks for your patience and understanding. We've just fixed a client-side bug that causes corrupted blockchain error when you restart wallet v1.3.0.0..."

On the 4th of August at 12:55:19 UTC, user "ReddCoin" said:

> "We just bought 1275$ worth of ads on Reddit to promote our new video.
>
> http://www.reddit.com/r/reddCoin/comments/2ckzwm/
> i_just_bought_some_reddit_ads_to_promote_our_new/"

Many members of the community were happy that funds were being directed towards active marketing of the coin. They viewed this as important to increase the awareness of Reddcoin, especially just after the implementation of proof of stake velocity. The first two responses to the purchase of advertisements on Reddit were made by "BitcoinBasics" and "RavenElite". They respectively said:

> "NOICE! (nice). Wow, pretty decent budget too.
> Looks like the right subreddits have been targeted, Nice Job."
>
> "Awesome!! I keep showing it to all my friends and sharing on Facebook :D"

One day later, user "bigreddmachine" on Bitcointalk described staking:

> "Staking is basically a lottery, just like mining. The more coins you have
> (and the longer you've had them), the more lottery tickets you have.
> There is a lottery held every minute for Reddcoin, so 1440 per day. That means 1440 stakes
> will earn interest. Given that there are a few thousand wallets as a minimum for RDD, and
> that most of them have multiple stakes based on
> transaction history, you have some stiff competition for winning. If you have really large
> stakes in a very big wallet, you could probably sync every once in a while and be fine. But if
> you have smaller stakes or a smaller wallet, you are
> going to want to run your wallet as often as possible to have the most
> opportunities at winning a stake.
>
> That applies for every PoS coin. Sometimes calling staking "interest" can be
> misleading because it makes it seem like everyone should have no trouble getting it. It's
> really a reward, and the amount of the reward is determined in a way
> similar to interest."

Since the announcement of a future social wallet on the 14th of June 2014, user "/u/hoppipoppipolla" had continued to work on its development. On the 7th of August at 08:49:33 UTC on the Reddcoin subreddit, user "/u/hoppipoppipolla" said:

"Hello Reddcoiners,

As some of you more seasoned reddcoiners may know, I have been working on a new wallet for Reddcoin! The day has finally come to release version 1.0.0.
Hopefully this will cheer you up from worrying about the price.

The social wallet incorporates all the functionality you'd expect from a normal wallet with extra features such as news, announcements and even chat so people can get help quickly in the friendly IRC channel #reddcoin.

This new wallet will allow us to slowly bridge the gap and integrate with the social web and the yet to be released Reddcoin Tipping Platform..."

A "#TipReddcoinWeek" was held to celebrate the successful launch of PoSV:

In the second half of the month, user "reddibrek" wrote three articles on Reddit about his personal thoughts on Reddcoin and cryptocurrencyin general. These articles were titled:

1.   A future for cryptocurrency?

2.   The zero-sum game vs wealth creation

3.   Reddcoin – zero-sum game or wealth creation?

An upgrade to the social wallet was released on the 25th of August. It was a bug fix release (v1.1.0) with two news features.

Two days later, both the social wallet (v1.1.1) and QT wallet client (v1.3.1.2) were upgraded. User "/u/hoppipoppipolla" said:

"Hey all!

This is a small bug fix release for Reddcoin core. I have also added some more information to the statistics page on the social wallet. You can find the download links here:

https://github.com/reddcoin-project/reddcoin/releases/tag/v1.3.1.2..."

On the last day of the month, user "bigreddmachine" joined the Reddcoin development team. He had accepted an offer from Laudney to create a wikipedia site devoted entirely to Reddcoin content. At the time, the site had already been set up at wiki.reddcoin.com . He admitted that the task was too much for him alone, so he asked members of the community to help add content to it.

Other events which occurred in the month of August were:

- On the 11th of August, Bitcointalk user "BRADLEYPLOOF" created a subreddit specifically for commenting on the price of Reddcoin (.../r/reddcoinpricewatch). Reddheads could now speculate about price without it occurring on the main Reddcoin subreddit.

- On the 18th of August, www.wesellredd.com had already sold a total of 240 million Reddcoin in the space of about three weeks.

- On the 25th of August, Reddcoin surpassed Litecoin in terms of the number of subscribers on Reddit.

SOCIAL X DETAILS ANNOUNCED

SEPTEMBER 2014

I.   Social X details were announced.

II.   Latest "#Tip Reddcoin Week" occurred to celebrate Social X details.

III.   QT Wallet v1.4 and Electrum Desktop Wallet v1.0.2 released.

IV.   Reddcoin went live on Pock.io.

V.   Community news website called www.reddheads.com revamped.

One month had now passed since the successful change from proof of work mining to a new innovative timestamping algorithm called proof of stake velocity. Since the 2nd of August 2014, the Reddcoin project had been in its second stage of active development. Stage one occurred up to the last day of PoW mining and had achieved a relatively fair coin distribution via the IPCO, tipping and mining. A team of highly skilled and trustworthy developers had also been attracted to the project.

Stage two of Reddcoin development had begun. It was time to devise strategies in order to make the utilisation of Reddcoin more friendly, less stressful and more socially rewarding to the average non-technical public user. Laudney named this period of Reddcoin development Social X. He cited three main problems for Social X to solve. These were increasing the ease with which one uses wallets , retaining full control of ones private keys and making tipping more socially acceptable.

Lead developer Laudney continued to describe the aspects of Social X being actively developed. These were the following:

1. Creating a thinner wallet (Electrum) that only requires a user to download a specific fraction of the blockchain (solves hefty blockchain downloads).

2. All wallets will permit the generation of private keys from passphrases. Being deterministic in nature, the passphrase will be all that is necessary to access and backup funds (solves the portability problem).

3. Generate public keys on demand while keeping private keys in cold storage (solves the cold storage problem).

4. A user will be able to associate a multitude of different names, addresses or emails to a certain private key. These names are then publicly known on the blockchain so others can easily send RDD to these. These will be known as Redd-IDs and will require annual re-registration to keep ownership of them.

5. A decentralised tipping platform that allows users to tip on social media sites such as Reddit or Twitter by sending RDD directly from local wallet to local wallet. This will then remove the need for trust in third-party centralised tipbot servers that run the risk of going down.

In conclusion, Social X is a continuously broad based plan, not a single project, in order to create an ecosystem in which users do not rely on third party exchanges, services and tipbots.

At the end of the blog article on the 6th of September , he concluded by saying:

"Below I'll only answer questions selectively. Much more details will be available in the whitepaper and there is no reason to jump the gun and repeat it here. Stage one took us 6 months. We expect stage two to take 6 months also. It may be the most exciting period in the history of Reddcoin project.

Regards

laudney"

One day after the announcement of Social X, the first payment processor called Litepaid (a shopping cart API provider) incorporated Reddcoin. At 02:24:45 UTC on Reddit, user "mastertrader777" described how it works:

"When the LitePaid API in your website or webshop has been integrated, you can start directly with receiving payments. While choosing a payment option on your website, the user will be send trough to the LitePaid Payment page."

In order for the community to celebrate the prior release of the Social X details, another "#TipReddcoinWeek" was scheduled beginning on the 8th of September to the 16th of September. On Reddheads.com, reddibrek said:

"It's time for Reddheads to get tipping across supported social networks!"

On the 21st of September, two wallets were released by the development team. These were:

- It was highly recommended that users upgraded to version 1.4 of the qt wallet client. It included numerous fixes and new features.

- Version 1.0.2 of the Electrum wallet for desktop was the first public release of this kind of wallet. It was made available on Windows, Mac and Linux.

In addition to the above two releases, a contest had begun to design interface icons for a future Electrum wallet. First prize was one million RDD.

On the first day of September, a tweet was sent from @reddcoin to @pockiouk:

> "Hey @pockiouk cool service you have there!
> Can you accept Reddcoin?"

Twenty two days later, Reddcoin went live on Pock.io. It is described as the easiest way for consumers in the UK to buy gift cards with cryptocurrency. It was added alongside other cryptocurrencies such as Bitcoin, Litecoin and Dogecoin. The service launched in early January 2014 and, by the middle of March, offered a total of eight accepted methods of cryptographic payment. On the 23rd of September, the site offered 156 different gift cards including Amazon, Google Play Store and Starbucks. A quote from the CEO and co-founder of Pock.io was:

> "I had the idea of gift cards even before I knew Gyft and other competitors were available.
> When I did my research, I obviously found them in the US market, but there was nothing in the UK.
> I saw a gap that not only I wanted to fill, but needed to be filled."

This service was rebranded to GiftOff in celebration of their first birthday. By the 9th of June 2015, the site offered 196 gift cards which can be purchased with one of twenty two cryptocurrencies. These are Bitcoin, BitcoinDark, Blackcoin, DigiByte, Dogecoin, Earthcoin, Feathercoin, HyperStake, Litecoin, Maxcoin, Namecoin, Peercoin, Primecoin, Quark, Reddcoin, Startcoin, Unobtanium, Vericoin, Vertcoin, Viacoin, Worldcoin and Zetacoin. There exists a zero commission fee on the site.

Throughout the second half of the month, the Reddcoin community website at www.reddheads.com was being revamped thanks to Reddibrek and some other members of the community. He was happy with all the help he had already received. The site would look more professional besides its increase in functionality as the official news site for Reddheads. A long term strategy had been devised to make the site more reliable, reputable and respected towards its target audience.

Reddibrek also notified the community of an upcoming newsletter service (planned to begin next month) and a competition to choose a new reddheads.com website logo had begun (closing date on the 28th of October 2014). At the end of Reddibrek's blog article on the 28th of September, he said:

"I am really grateful to have been given the opportunity to be chief editor of Reddheads.com, and I look forward to helping the website to grow and develop to become an informative, dynamic and exciting source of news. It gives me great pleasure to invite Reddcoin community members to submit any articles or synopses to this address: editorial@reddheads.com.

As Reddcoin continues to grow and the user-base extends around the world, the workload for the website will surely increase. Please feel free to volunteer assistance at any time if you feel like you may be able to help.

If you have any comments or questions you can make them below or send me an e-mail."

On the penultimate day of September, both a Facebook group and Twitter page for Reddheads.com were created.

The vast majority of daily trading volume continued to occur on Cryptsy. On the last day of September, the price of one unit of Reddcoin account was in the range 12-15 BTC Satoshi and that day's RRD/BTC trading volume was 93.1766 BTC on this exchange.

OFFICIAL BLOCK EXPLORER, WIKIPEDIA AND NEWSLETTER RELEASED

OCTOBER 2014

I.   Official Reddcoin block explorer launched.

II. Issue one of the official Reddcoin newsletter published.

III. Interview between Laudney and Reddibrek.

IV. Reddcoin social wallet v1.4.0 released.

V.   Reddcoin Wikipedia ready for action.

On the 2nd of October, Reddcoin began trading on the exchange CCEDK as multiple trading pairs including RDD/BTC, RDD/LTC and RDD/USD.

Also on the second day of the month, the official Reddcoin block explorer became available at http://live.reddcoin.com/. On the homepage of this explorer one can easily see the latest timestamped blocks and transactions. A search bar at the top of the page permits one to easily find a specific block, transaction or wallet address. On Bitcointalk, "bigreddmachine" announced this at 23:39:51 UTC. He said:

"Just wanted everyone to know about the new Reddcoin block explorer and API, based off of Bitpay's Bitcore & Insight API:

live.reddcoin.com"

Members of the Reddcoin community were notified of the upcoming publication of the first Reddcoin newsletter on the 4th of October. This notification was titled "Reddheads newsletter - exclusive content coming". Reddibrek at 09:12:03 UTC said:

> "I will soon send out the first Reddheads newsletter. As I said in the recent Reddheads post (http://redd.it/2hpmw8) outlining the vision and future plans for the website, newsletters will contain exclusive content.
> It is very much in the interests of every Reddcoin community member to sign up!
> You can do so on the homepage of www.reddheads.com."

On the 8th of October 2014, the official Reddcoin newsletter made its debut. Issue one was released titled "Welcome to the newsletter!" by community member Reddibrek, Chief Editor. In the newsletter, he said:

> "What better way to mark the first Reddheads.com newsletter than some words from the Reddcoin Lead Developer. I put a few questions to Laudney about the new blockchain explorer and APIs Reddsight, and couldn't resist asking about Social X.
>
> The Reddheads mailing list has just been launched. As time goes by the newsletter will increase in size, with a range of unique content and key insights into the Reddcoin project. The editorial team is enthusiastic and we look forward to keeping you informed!"

A full transcript of the interview between Laudney and Reddibrek is in the appendix of this book.

On the 10th of October, after some delay, an upgrade of the Reddcoin social wallet (a.k.a. ReddWallet) was released. More specifically, it was the release of version 1.4.0. Supported platforms included Windows, Linux (32 and 64-bit) and Mac OS X. On the official Reddcoin blog, Laudney went on to say:

> "We have fixed several bugs and most importantly updated reddcoind daemon to 1.4.0.0. However, a few Mac users may run into problems of running the wallet due to some stability issues in the frameworks used by our implementation (nodewebkit).
>
> I'd suggest these Mac users switch back to the Qt wallet for the time being.
>
> Going forward, the social wallet will be completely rewritten and become the official Electrum wallet for desktop."

On the 14th of October, the second issue of the Reddcoin newsletter was released titled "Dencentralisation by "redducation"".

As introduced in late August, the new Reddcoin Wiki initiative by Bigreddmachine had progressed greatly. By the 19th of October, a significant amount of content had been added to the site since its inception. These were:

- An introduction to Reddcoin.

- A history of Reddcoin.

- Pages on proof of work, proof of stake and proof of stake velocity.

- A page about Social X.

- A page about the Reddcoin development team.

Bigreddmachine also said that the process of translating specific pages into other languages had already started. He asked if anyone could help in this regard. Many thanks were made to all who had helped with the site up until this time.

In the third newsletter on the 22nd of October, one member of the Reddcoin developer team called "Bigreddmachine" was interviewed. The following is only the beginning of that interview, but the rest can be found at the link below:

Name:	Bigreddmachine / Mike
Age:	26
Nationality:	American
Day job:	Researcher/Aerospace Engineer
Programming languages / fluent:	Matlab, HTML/CSS
Programming languages / conversational:	Fortran, Python
Programming languages / learning:	Javascript

Time working on Reddcoin:

"I have been part of the community since late February 2014. My first venture into working on Reddcoin was as a content creator and moderator of the wiki page on /r/reddcoin sometime in Spring 2014. I officially joined the development team in late August 2014."

Responsibilities on the Reddcoin team:

"I am the chief editor and admin of wiki.reddcoin.com and help on other projects when I am able and have time. For example, I recently helped with the initial porting of Bitcore/Insight-API to Reddcore/Reddsight-API, and the front-end of the Reddsight block explorer."

Reasons for joining Reddcoin:

"I first got started with Reddcoin when the subreddit only had 2000 subscribers. I liked the goal of the project, and thought it would be cool to be part of something from nearly the beginning. I joined the development team because there was a need for a person to lead the Wiki project and I was approached by Laudney to take on the job."

http://us9.campaign-archive2.com/?
u=f660942d5df0331d9b0a3a3b9&id=bcd6c4e9b0&e=%5bUNIQID

On the 24th of October, user "ReddCoin" at 14:25:01 UTC said:

> "For all your wallet problems, check the green section.
> https://wiki.reddcoin.com/index.php/Troubleshooting
>
> Reddcoin"

On the 27th October at 17:03:09 UTC, Bigreddmachine, in response to forum users on Bitcointalk questioning when Social X would be complete, said:

> "It sounds to me like you do not fully understand the scope of Social X. It is a multi-project phase in Reddcoin's development, not a single product itself.
> As is very easy to find in this thread, the whitepaper has been pushed back and actual development is taking front stage at this moment.
> Please read these two resources if you want to understand Social X better:
>
> https://wiki.reddcoin.com/index.php/Social_X - Full summary of the phase and scope
> http://www.reddit.com/r/reddCoin/comments/2fncbj/
> social_x_architecture_of_a_decentralised_system/ - announcement of basic Social X details"

Another event which occurred in the month of October was:

- A new Reddcoin fan site was launched on the 11th of October at the website www.reddcoin.co.uk . This site no longer exists. A newsletter (Issue 4) published on the 29th of October discussed this new website.

NEW REDDCOIN SERVICES

NOVEMBER 2014

I.   Review of the last two months.

II.   User "usernameNotLongEnoug" was interviewed.

III.   Many Reddcoin faucets now available.

IV.   Reddcoin-only e-com store went live.

V.   New services based on Reddsight (Reddcoin Rocks and Reddrealm).

Hundreds of hours of voluntary work had been done by the Reddcoin development team over the past two months. This had contributed to the successful completion of the following aspects of the Reddcoin project:

1)   Electrum server deployment and desktop wallets.

2)   Official blockchain API and block explorer.

3)   Release of Qt wallet 1.4.0 and social wallet 1.4.0.

4)   Official launch of wiki site.

5)   Official re-launch of reddheads.com and community newsletter.

6)   Supported by major gift card merchant pock.io.

7)   Supported by payment processor litepaid.com.

At the end of the announcement about Reddcoin's progress on the 3rd of November at 21:23:20 UTC on Reddit, Laudney said:

> "The best way to predict the future is to create it.
> The Reddcoin Project is still an infant and the community is a huge part of it.
> Together we can create a future with exciting possibilities."

Two days later, issue number five of the official Reddcoin newsletter was published. It covered the recent progress of the coin as well as the personal perspective of Reddibrek, the chief editor of Reddheads.com. His closing comments at the end of the newsletter were:

> "When it comes to the future of the project, personally I am firmly in the "long-term view" camp. With a team of such trustworthy, dedicated and qualified people involved, such a great community (more and more of whom are launching their own Reddcoin games and services) and such a huge amount of potential out there, I feel fully secure looking into next year as I plan how I will maintain and develop my own involvement with Reddcoin. But for those of you for whom a week may seem like an eternity, I have a final anecdote. In the comments to Laudney's post, Reddcoin dev userNameNotLongEnoug was quizzed about the upcoming Electrum browser wallet (a cornerstone of the next generation tip platform, as you have already read). He narrowed down the time frame as he gave his views on the upcoming wallet:"
>
> "It will be worth the wait. I believe this will make reddcoin so easy to use that anyone can do it. All that's standing in the way is about 60 hours of programming"

On the 12th of November, an article was written on www.coincryptonews.com titled "Reddcoin Price Continues to Fall" by Josiah Wilmoth. It described how the price had fallen from its peak on the 27th of July to a Bitcoin Satoshi value of 13 on the last day of October. At the time of this article, Reddcoin had a market capitalisation of just above one million dollars.

Also on this day, the sixth issue of the newsletter was published in which another member of the team was interviewed (see opposite page).

Name: usernameNotLongEnoug / tralf / Andrew

Age: 26

Nationality: American

Day job: PHP and Javascript development. A bit of Linux administration. Occasionally I get to use Python for something small.

Programming languages/fluent: Javascript, PHP

Programming languages/conversational: Python, Java

Programming languages/learning: C++

Time working on Reddcoin: I published the first version of the first generation tip platform on April 5th, 2014 in response to a bounty. I later joined the project in a more official sense in early August.

Responsibilities on the Reddcoin team: My current (and most fun) job within Reddcoin is developing an Electrum Wallet that will run directly in the browser to make spending and receiving Reddcoin easier than ever. I have worked on some parts of the new and upcoming tip platform, and I help out with front-end web dev and NodeJs dev whenever I'm needed.

Reasons for joining Reddcoin: I was initially attracted to Reddcoin upon discovering that the team had a solid vision and a great work ethic. It was clear to me from the start that Reddcoin is a long-term project – a refreshing change from many of the pump and dump schemes popping up on a daily basis. After releasing the first gen tip platform I saw an appreciation of my efforts that I hadn't seen in any other coin and I knew I had found the place for me. But, to be honest, I mostly joined because I thought I would be invited to Laudney's yacht parties with free scotch and sushi. It's been a huge disappointment in that regard.

In issue seven of the official newsletter on the 19th of November, Reddibrek announced the launch of the Reddcoin-only e-commerce store called Reddibrek's (https://www.reddibreks.com). It offers a range of coffee, chilli and Belgian chocolate which can only be bought with Reddcoin. He said the store is an independent personal endeavour. He concluded the announcement by saying:

> "We have achieved our goal of getting Reddibrek's up and running for Christmas. But going beyond Christmas we have a conceived a detailed business plan that includes, among other things, increasing the size of the catalogue, offering new ranges of quality products and shipping to more destinations. But perhaps the most important part of the plan for the future is the integration of the new, cutting-edge Reddcoin functionality that is being developed under the project name Social X. We have built and will continue to build the store around Reddcoin as we believe that by doing this we will remain at the forefront of a new paradigm in e-commerce. For example, features such as Redd-ID will allow us to offer our customers a new way of managing an account with the store, while maintaining the streamlined model we have set up."

Three days later, two further services had been added to the Reddcoin ecosystem based on the Reddcoin block explorer and API service, Reddsight-api.

On the 22nd of November, subreddit user /u/stffn announced the availability of Reddcoin Rocks, a "simple website to keep track of staking rewards and balances". This site also shows the real time BTC/USD price from bitstamp and the RDD/BTC price from Cryptsy.

On the 23rd of November, subreddit user iisurge released the first section of his website Reddrealm (explorers.reddrealm.co). It is a simple block explorer, but no longer exists now. User iisurge was quoted as saying:

> "I am sorry to say ReddRealm
> (at least as it was originally planed) has been cancelled.
> The main reasoning for this being due to recent family events. I wasn't online much for a little over a month besides on mobile devices because of this.
> After being back I was thinking about ReddRealm and thought that it would not be used much besides maybe when it first launches..."

According to the site www.cryptocoincharts.info, the Bitcoin Satoshi values of one RDD unit of account and the trading volume on the last day of November were:

	Price (BTC Satoshi)	Low (BTC Satoshi)	Open (BTC Satoshi)	Close (BTC Satoshi)	High (BTC Satoshi)	Volume (BTC Satoshi)
Cryptsy	10.5	10	10	11	11	2.2173
Bittrex	11	10	11	11	11	0.58603
Poloniex	9	9	9	9	11	0.084995
Bleutrade	9.5	9	9	10	10	0.0017487
Swisscex	10	10	10	10	10	0.00033

Other events which occurred in the month of November were:

- CryptFolio began to support Reddcoin on the 7th of November. It is a site that allows one to keep track of one's cryptocurrencies, miners, investments and equities, and generates regular portfolio reports.

- User "bigreddmachine" on Bitcointalk directed the community towards the current list of Reddcoin faucets at the address http://freereddcoins.net on the 15th of November.

- Issue eight of the official newsletter was published on the 26th of November. It was titled "Raising Reddroom". It discussed the subject of online Poker.

- On the 27th of November, a service for shortening URL addresses was made available at http://rdd.pw.

REDDCOINTALK.ORG FORUM LAUNCHED

DECEMBER 2014

I.   Browser wallet demo video published.

II.   Reddcoin official forum at www.reddcointalk.org launched.

III.   Reddcoin Bitcointalk thread closed.

IV.   ShapeShift added Reddcoin to their platform.

V.   Browser wallet public beta released.

It had been known that development of a thinner wallet (electrum browser wallet) was in progress. User "usernameNotLongEnoug" (tralf) had been very busy creating it since it was announced as one of the major future milestones of Social X back in September. Last month, he took part in an interview for the Reddheads newsletter in which he confirmed his work on the project (see page 103). This work would underpin the future decentralised peer-to-peer tip platform.

On the 2nd of December, a video preview of the browser wallet was uploaded to YouTube at https://www.youtube.com/watch?v=hjsgIa5rrIg. Praise was given for his hard work:

> "The Reddheads team congratulates tralf and the Reddcoin team on the results of their tireless efforts to develop and maintain Reddcoin's status as an innovative and cutting-edge cryptocurrency project... with a long-term vision!"

In the ninth issue of the Reddcoin newsletter on the 3rd of December titled "Wallets take centre stage", another member of the team was interviewed. The first part of the interview is shown on the adjacent page.

One week later, the tenth newsletter was published. It was titled "Highlights of an amazing year". It listed the achievements during the year 2014:

- The Initial Public Coin Offering (IPCO).
- The logo went through a process of redesign.
- A plethora of "traditional" wallets and a unique Reddcoin social wallet.
- The launch of a host of official websites including for example www.reddcoin.com and the community site www.reddheads.com.
- Reddcoin Broadcast.
- The Reddcoin tip platform, covering Reddit, Twitter and Twitch TV, was released to overwhelmingly positive reviews.
- Reddcoin's Lead Dev Larry Ren published his PoSV White Paper.
- The implementation of PoSV.
- The creation of the Reddcoin Wiki.
- Announcement of the next major phase in the Reddcoin project, Social X.
- The launch of a block explorer and official APIs, Reddsight.
- The release of Reddcoin Electrum wallets, as the initial stage of Social X.
- More Social X in the form of a video teaser showing the cornerstone of the next generation tipping platform in an advanced stage of development.

108

Name:	raid5 / Adam McDonald
Age:	30
Nationality:	American
Education:	BS / MS in Computer Science
Programming languages / fluent:	Objective-C, Ruby, Java
Programming languages / conversational:	Python, Javascript
Programming languages / learning:	Go

Experience: I started my professional career when I was an undergrad. In one of the computer science classes I attended, our professor was so impressed with the end result of our class project that he spun it out into a startup company with a few of us students. I was mainly doing backend enterprise Java and frontend web development at the time. Once mobile platforms started to emerge, I was quick to jump on learning both iOS and Android development. I now work for an agency that focuses on design/development of mobile, set-top, and tv apps.

Time working on Reddcoin: I've been involved with Reddcoin development for a couple months now.

Responsibilities on the Reddcoin team: My main focus has been laying down the foundation and UI for the upcoming iOS wallet.

Reasons for joining Reddcoin: I got into cryptocurrencies in late 2013 as a miner. Bitcoin, Litecoin, and Dogecoin were my main areas of interest initially since they were the big players. When Reddcoin was officially announced, I immediately knew this project had potential. I lurked around the subreddit for a while and eventually started getting more and more involved. We have a great dev team and I'm always looking forward to the awesome stuff they do.

http://us9.campaign-archive2.com/?
u=f660942d5df0331d9b0a3a3b9&id=d8a877b9e4

On the 14th of December at 18:45:48 UTC, Laudney announced on Reddit that a brand new official community forum for Reddcoin had been launched. He said that all future announcements concerning the coin will occur here before on any other social media discussion site such as Facebook, Reddit or Twitter. A giveaway was created soon after its creation. New members who register an account on the forum would receive 10,000 RDD by posting their wallet address (public key) in the appropriate thread. The URL link of the forum is www.reddcointalk.org.

Shortly after the official forum went live, the Reddcoin thread on Bitcointalk closed. The discussion about Reddcoin had already been shifting away from Bitcointalk since the late summer of 2014. This thread had been active from the 20th of January 2014 for a total of 329 days. The final post on the thread was made by "ReddCoin" on the 15th of December at 01:55:16 UTC. He said:

> "This topic is closed.
>
> Join us at ReddcoinTalk.org to continue the discussion.
>
> https://www.reddcointalk.org
>
> thanks
> Reddcoin"

It is still possible to read the whole thread, but nobody now can reply to anyone's prior posted comments.

On the 24th of December, Reddcoin was added to the instant cryptocurrency conversion platform called Shape Shift. Established in August 2014, it is a Swiss web platform. It allows users to instantly convert one cryptocurrency into another without creating an account or depositing funds. Erik Voorhees is the founder and CEO. On the 16th of June 2015, there were a total of thirty five different coins accepted. Charlie Lee, the founder of Litecoin, was quoted as saying:

> "I've been waiting for a service like this. Great job!"

According to the site www.cryptocoincharts.info, the Bitcoin Satoshi values of one RDD unit of account and the trading volume on the last day of the year 2015 were:

	Price (BTC Satoshi)	Low (BTC Satoshi)	Open (BTC Satoshi)	Close (BTC Satoshi)	High (BTC Satoshi)	Volume (BTC Satoshi)
Cryptsy	12	11	11	13	13	19.3268
Bittrex	11	11	11	11	13	0.426189
Poloniex	12.5	12	12	13	13	0.590969
Bleutrade	11	10	10	12	12	0.013496
Swisscex	11.5	11	11	12	12	0.0313399

In terms of an approximate US Dollar price, the average value of one unit of RDD account was about $0.000037. This equates roughly to 27,027 RDD per $1 (average obtained from the website www.bitinfocharts.com).

Other events which occurred in the month of December were:

- On the 7th of December, Reddcoin began live trading on the exchange called Cryptopia. Initial trading pairs included RDD/BTC, RDD/LTC and RDD/DOGE

- Laudney wrote an article in which he supported the need for Reddcoin to have an official mascot. The article was posted on the 10th of December.

- On the 17th of December, the last newsletter of 2014 was published titled "Building The Social Currency". It was written early (before the holidays) as the first newsletter of 2015.

- On the 22nd of December, reddcoin.rocks initiated audio notifications.

- On the 25th of December, the beta browser wallet of Reddcoin was publicly released.

- On the 26th of December, Reddcoin began live trading on the exchange called Cryptoine. It closed down on the last day of April 2015.

REDDCOIN LTD ANNOUNCED

JANUARY 2015

I.   Is 2015 the year of Reddcoin adoption?

II.   Long blocks intervals noticed on the Reddcoin network.

III.   QT wallet and reddcoind v1.4.1.0 released.

IV.   Reddcoin Ltd announced as established.

V.   One year since block number one was mined.

January 2015 was the first month to begin without any Reddcoin community discussion on the recently closed official Reddcoin Bitcointalk thread. Nevertheless, discussion had always been occurring on other social media sites such as Reddit and had begun on the recently created official Reddcoin forum (www.reddcointalk.org).

On the 7th of January 2015, after the Christmas holidays, an article was written on reddheads.com titled "Reddcoin 2015—year of adoption". Reddibrek and the Reddheads Team were happy to be back. One of the main events to look forward to was the next generation Reddcoin tipping platform. With greater functionality and ease of use, a lot of hard work was being put into developing the code thanks to professional computer science programmers. Reddibrek was also clear in his continued aspiration for Reddcoin. He said the community must maintain accounts with the most important social networks.

Within the first week or so of January, there were long blocks intervals on the Reddcoin network. There were accusations that the network had collapsed, but this claim was refuted by Laudney who was quoted as saying:

"First, it's incorrect to say the Reddcoin network is *down*. The network works as it should: nodes relay block and transaction information to each other and most importantly all the nodes on the network agree on one single longest chain, which is the cornerstone of our decentralised network. There is no magic switch to turn our decentralised network *off* or *on*. Being a truly decentralised crypto-currency is what Reddcoin Project is all about.

Second, *minting* a block is an action carried out by each staking node (*staker*) *independently*. All the information required to create a coinstake transaction and its corresponding PoSV block is available locally after being relayed on the network. When hundreds or thousands of stakers compete to mint the next block, there is no coordination required among them. Not only no coordination, it's actually a fierce competition in nature."

Reasons why long block intervals occurred could have been due to some Reddcoin stakers temporarily going offline or a software bug in the qt wallet client. At the time of the above comment by Laudney, he was still on an undisclosed business trip. He said he would investigate the issue further once he had returned in the following week.

Also on the 9th of January, Laudney announced that he was finalising the technical details of PoSV 2.0 which will distribute the interests given up by inactive wallets to active stakers. This will be included as part of the Social X release together with a corresponding new design document.

On the 12th of January, a new build release was made available (v1.4.1.0) with thanks to help from @Gnasher. Lead developer Laudney urged all users, especially those involved in staking RDD, to upgrade as soon as possible. This upgrade was not mandatory due to a future fork in the blockchain, only a fix to the code. This was the fix required as a result of the long bloated block times discovered three days previously.

On the 14th of January, the source code of the Reddcoin social wallet was made freely open source under GNU Licence v2. Laudney welcomed members of the Reddcoin community to read, study and improve upon this code. Also on this day, issue 13, or the third newsletter of 2015, was published by Reddibrek. It was titled "Broad Trends in Cryptocurrency. The start of the article is as follows:

"While the primary goal of the Reddheads newsletter is to provide information, interviews and articles specifically about the Reddcoin project, it is also a publication that aims to give some perspective on cryptocurrency in general. Hence the focus in this week's issue on broad trends that are set to have a long-term impact on the future of cryptocurrency.

In the beginning...

To grasp the whole context, one has to start at the beginning. And in the beginning, there was Bitcoin. What was it about Bitcoin that was considered to be genuine innovation?

Bitcoin (or rather, the blockchain) is a solution to the "Byzantine Generals" problem of consensus between nodes when faced with the possibility of bad actors and other issues. This problem may be relevant to financial transactions but also to identity verification, contract validation, etc. Up until now, in many cases the solution to the problem has been simply to avoid it: for example, VISA keeps track of financial transactions by controlling a central ledger; VISA does not require consensus with itself.

With the invention of the blockchain came the decentralised ledger: distributed consensus, intended to be controlled by no-one..."

A big announcement was made at the beginning of 2015. A public limited company (PLC) called Reddcoin Ltd was established by the founder and lead developer of Reddcoin on the 20th of October 2014. The founding of this legal entity was viewed as a great step forward for the Reddcoin project. According to the website http://www.datalog.co.uk, the details of this company are :

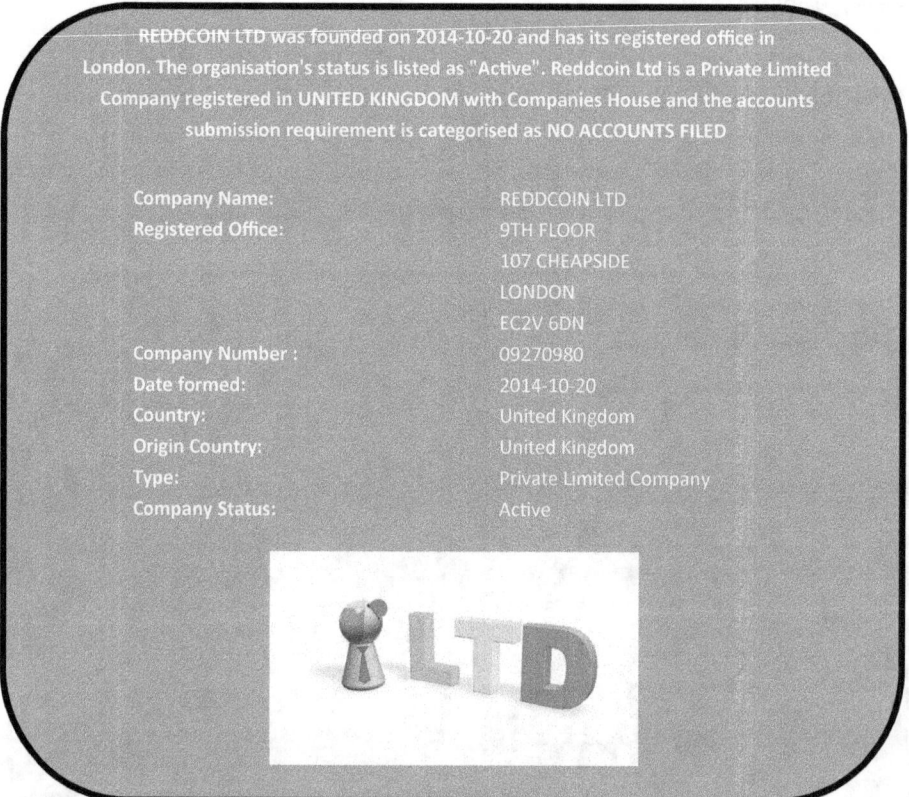

REDDCOIN LTD was founded on 2014-10-20 and has its registered office in London. The organisation's status is listed as "Active". Reddcoin Ltd is a Private Limited Company registered in UNITED KINGDOM with Companies House and the accounts submission requirement is categorised as NO ACCOUNTS FILED

Company Name:	REDDCOIN LTD
Registered Office:	9TH FLOOR
	107 CHEAPSIDE
	LONDON
	EC2V 6DN
Company Number :	09270980
Date formed:	2014-10-20
Country:	United Kingdom
Origin Country:	United Kingdom
Type:	Private Limited Company
Company Status:	Active

On the 26th of January, the blockchain was officially one year old. A total of 516,490 blocks had been generated before block number 516,491 was timestamped at 21:32:03 UTC (see adjacent page). Considering that there were 365 days in 2014, each block took about 61.058 seconds on average to generate. As a reminder, the IPCO pre-mine was mined from block numbers one to ten before the public release of the blockchain on the 2nd of February 2014.

Block #516490

BlockHash 1ea1a299debb5ca18f7ec00f2bf5a9a1d04c33d44c29c070e458d6599b1cf79ec

Summary

Number Of Transactions	2	Difficulty	293.65318691
Height	516490 (Mainchain)	Bits	1c00df05
Block Type	PoSV	Size (bytes)	444
Block Reward	0 RDD	Version	3
Timestamp	Jan 26, 2015 9:31:27 PM	Nonce	0
Merkle Root	5da5e18d1fae36b68d44b53c40054b7..	Next Block	516491
Previous Block	516489		

Block #516491

BlockHash 9bf139c5ba9439af2a59ef3a49c6452080d6e6b35a70033cccc57d6435e4b182tt0

Summary

Number Of Transactions	4	Difficulty	293.99737142
Height	516491 (Mainchain)	Bits	1c00dee9
Block Type	PoSV	Size (bytes)	907
Block Reward	0 RDD	Version	3
Timestamp	Jan 26, 2015 9:32:03 PM	Nonce	0
Merkle Root	97650c5c400bbb66041 23e40954255f	Next Block	516492
Previous Block	516490		

REDDCOIN ONE YEAR ANNIVERSARY

FEBRUARY 2015

I.   Reddcoin one year old at block 526,012.

II.   Comkort began to trade Reddcoin on their exchange.

III.   Reddcoin prices on the 2nd of February 2015.

IV.   Reddcoin daily trading volumes on the 2nd of February 2015.

V.   Reddheads article for Reddcoin's birthday published

On the 2nd of February 2015, the Reddcoin blockchain successfully reached its one year anniversary since the community had been able to either mine or stake Reddcoin via proof of work mining or proof of stake velocity minting respectively. As can be seen on the page 121, block number 526,012 marked the time at which this happened. At this block, 885.99843217 RDD were staked. On the official Reddcoin Twitter page, the following tweet was posted:

> "Reddcoin turns 1-year-old today, Happy birthday!"

In addition to the above milestone, Reddcoin began trading on the exchange called Comkort (Estonia) on the same day. This exchange opened for beta testing on the 20th of February 2014 before it went fully operational in early March 2014. Three trading pairs (RDD/BTC, RDD/LTC and RDD/DOGE) were initially made available.

According to the site www.cryptocoincharts.info, the closing Bitcoin Satoshi values of one RDD unit of account and the trading volumes on the 2nd of February were:

	Price (BTC Satoshi)	Low (BTC Satoshi)	Open (BTC Satoshi)	Close (BTC Satoshi)	High (BTC Satoshi)	Volume (BTC Satoshi)
Cryptsy	9	9	9	9	11	8.53057
Bittrex	10	9	10	10	11	1.23799
Poloniex	10	10	10	10	10	0.139334
Bleutrade	9	9	9	9	11	0.0373431
Swisscex	12	10	14	10	14	0.0007114

An article was written by Reddibrek on the 6th of February titled "Reddcoin 1 year old this week". It discussed the first year of Bitcoin, the Euro and Reddcoin. For Reddcoin, the following was written:

Reddcoin – 1st birthday / public release 2 February 2014

"Reddcoin was launched at a time when the cryptocurrency scene was blooming following the huge mainstream attention paid to Bitcoin at the end of 2013. One year on and the majority of the diverse cryptocurrency projects set in motion in 2014 have faded away and been resigned to crypto-history.

Thanks to its team and dedicated community Reddcoin is one of the few projects that continues to forge ahead with innovation and promise for the future.

At the end of 2014 Reddheads published an astonishing résumé of Reddcoin's progress and development over the year."

Block #526012

BlockHash be106be2aaca12d19c69e4c934ae776f0da04f9e84f3b142b1b804337Oeb61B430

Summary

Number Of Transactions	6	Difficulty	211.82227946
Height	526012 (Mainchain)	Bits	1c013563
Block Type	PoSV	Size (bytes)	6016
Block Reward	0 RDD	Version	3
Timestamp	Feb 2, 2015 3:54:06 PM	Nonce	0
Merkle Root	00e7f00e6e2af6688de109236ed0ae...	Next Block	526013
Previous Block	526011		

121

APPENDIX

APPENDIX

INTERVIEW BETWEEN DREW CORDELL AND LAUDNEY PUBLISHED ON THE 21ST OF MARCH 2014

What is your name and position at Reddcoin?

"My name is @laudney, and I'm a core developer for the Reddcoin project."

What duties do you do for the coin on a daily basis?

"I'm involved in many aspects of the project. I talk with other core and active members daily through emails, conference calls and IRC chat. My main focus is on building and running the core infrastructure systems for Reddcoin. I'm the author of Reddcoin tipbots for Twitter, Twitch.tv and Justin.tv. I run these bots on cloud servers and monitor them on a daily basis. I maintain the Reddcoin Github repository, and I'm writing several new systems. I also spend a lot of time interacting with the community on /r/reddcoin.

I do all of these in my very limited spare time (< five hours a day) because I have a full-time job."

What are the current projects you are working on?

"I'm working on many things. The top of my list is a website that describes the state of the Reddcoin economy in real-time. It'll calculate and display many statistics, analogous to economic indicators, that give people an overview of the state of the economy. Statistics include the number of tips across different social networks, the top tippers, the top receivers and many more. I want everyone to have a very clear picture of what's happening in the Reddcoin economy, down to the very tipping transactions. We will also use it to monitor the effectiveness of our marketing and PR campaigns. It'll be a very useful tool to quantify various aspects of the Reddcoin ecosystem and that's why I've decided to work on this before everything else such as more tip bots."

What do you feel makes this crypto-currency unique?

"To answer this question properly, I need to first give a quick overview of the crypto -currency world based on my own understanding. This will be a long answer so please bear with me.

I divide all the crypto-currencies into four categories. The first category includes Bitcoin and to a less extent Litecoin. They are technologically mature and are well into the phase of building out real-world businesses.

The second category includes altcoins whose selling points are mainly technical. Most of them use modified hashing algorithms which offer limited real-life benefits in the economic sense. A few of them are more innovative by proposing and implementing new features in the blockchain to enable new features such as improved anonymity.

The third category includes all the pump-and-dump-ponzi-scheme altcoins. Unfortunately they make up the vast majority of the altcoin universe and come out everyday. They are created by a small group of people as tools to facilitate wealth transfer in deceptive fashion. Altcoin markets are arguably the freest market in the world. They are unregulated and brutal. They are truly zero-sum games (or even negative-sum games after taking into account transaction costs). People playing the games all think "I'm smarter than the average guy." and they all forget that "price is what you pay; value is what you get." To quote Warren Buffett, "Only when the tide goes out do you discover who's been swimming naked."

The last category includes Dogecoin and Reddcoin. These two are unique in the sense that their economy and ecosystem are mostly driven by the community. Dogecoin, starting from a joke and heavily relying on meme, broke many new grounds in the altcoin world. Their community's ability to organize various social activities is very impressive. Having said that, I do believe Dogecoin has some inherent flaws. I don't want to openly criticize it and refer you to a FAQ named "Reddcoin vs Doge".

So, what makes Reddcoin unique? There are many reasons but let me just point out a few. First, Reddcoin had a successful IPOC. The funding is being actively and cautiously deployed to build out the core pieces of the infrastructure and fund marketing campaigns. The huge advantage of the central funding is often neglected and understated. Second, Reddcoin was created with a clear vision to be _the_ social currency. Its design is professional and appeals to real-life merchants and businesses. Third, Reddcoin, at the moment, is _the_ fastest growing community in the entire crypto-currency world. The number of subscribers in /r/reddcoin is growing exponentially. The number of tweets with hashtag #Reddcoin is growing exponentially. Fourth, Reddcoin attracts some of the best people into the community, usually ones who are serious, passionate, patient and hardworking. This speaks a lot about the Reddcoin brand."

What do you want to see more of from the community?
What can we as the community do to aid the development of this currency?

"I answer these two questions together. In short, I hope everyone in the community can add value to the Reddcoin ecosystem in any way possible. Everyone has different skill sets and can contribute in their unique ways.

Less than 1% of the community are ones who are able to develop, from graphics, stickers, browser plugins, websites to bots and more complicated infrastructure. If you are one of them, please do come forward and volunteer and share your proud work with all of us. There are bounties for some of the core pieces.

These numbers may seem low, but they are still way higher than almost all the other altcoins out there. However given Reddcoin's vision to become the social currency, we want to see more passive members come forward and contribute. If you have an idea, don't be shy; share it with us; discuss it with us. If you have made something cool for Reddcoin, come and show us. All your efforts will be greatly appreciated."

Where do you see Reddcoin in two years?

"Reddcoin will still be here in two years, and it'll be the ultimate validation of the vision and efforts of the community. In an altcoin world where lifetime is measured in months if not weeks, being able to survive two years is the very definition of success itself.

So where do I see Reddcoin in two years? I hope to see Reddcoin popularise crypto-currencies among the general public and become deeply ingrained in every aspect of people's social lives. Santoshi admitted himself that Bitcoin is not practical for micropayment. Reddcoin is well-suited to fill this gap. I also know there is a huge amount of work for everyone. The road is long and in the end the journey is the destination."

Which social media outlets do you think are most important for the growth of Reddcoin?

"None and all of them. One by one we will bring each social network into the Reddcoin economy. Having said that, I do want to mention that we see huge potential and opportunity for Reddcoin in China."

What are the major current goals of infrastructure for Reddcoin?

"First and foremost, we are working on cloud-hosted APIs (credit to @ReddAPI) that deal with all the complexity and security issues related to creating user wallets, making payment and maintaining balances so that developers can focus on building 3rd-party applications such as merchant tools and online shops.

We are working on the website for Reddcoin economy as mentioned before, and infographics for Reddcoin.

Later on I'll release more tip bots for various social networks. We'll also look at adding new features to the Reddcoin blockchain to support "financial contracts' that open up all sorts of possibilities like a subscription (i.e. recurring payment), escrow, auction and interest-bearing debt.

Finally, I'd like to reiterate the importance of Chinese market to Reddcoin. China is responsible for over 50% of global trading volume of crypto-currencies and enjoys a vibrant and fast-developing industry. We are working on long-term strategic partnership with Chinese Internet companies to both develop infrastructure and promote Reddcoin as the ultimate social currency for the world's most populous country. It's also interesting to note that red is the favorite color of the country so Reddcoin's Chinese name could prove to be a big hit."

INTERVIEW BETWEEN REDDIBREK AND LAUDNEY PUBLISHED ON THE 8TH OF OCTOBER 2014

RH: Congratulations on the launch of the Reddsight block explorer and APIs. Who worked on this part of the Reddcoin project?

Laudney: /u/bigreddmachine and /u/userNameNotLongEnoug worked on the front end and styling. I worked on PoSV-specific data structures and core logic.

RH: Why was this new service developed and released "under the radar"?

Laudney: In addition to the main branch of development as described in the official roadmap, we also have several side projects that provide relatively minor but still important pieces to the overall "jigsaw puzzle". An official blockchain explorer and APIs have been internally considered for some time. Recently the community explicitly requested it so we felt the time was right to bring it to fruition.

RH: Please could you give a couple of examples of how APIs could be used?

Laudney: The APIs are very comprehensive. They provide even morefunctionalities than RPC calls built into reddcoind. /u/BrownSlaughter is already using them to build a new version of the RddCompanion browser extension that allows users to see the balance of addresses and how long it takes to stake, without need for a wallet. One can also use it to build wallets or reporting tools that show interesting statistics of the Reddcoin blockchain. With a bit of work, one can also implement payment services for e-commerce.

It's also useful to note that one can actually set up and host these APIs on their own servers if they so desire. There is detailed documentation at https://github.com/reddcoin-project/reddsight-api

RH: How many other cryptocurrency projects provide this level of functionality?

Laudney: Recently Bitcoin has seen several startups provide cloud-based APIs. You can read about them here:

http://www.coindesk.com/cex-io-joins-bitcoin-api-race-launch-plugchain/
A couple of them also support Litecoin and Dogecoin mainly due to the fact that all of them are PoW and therefore code change required is minimal. To my best knowledge, Reddcoin is the first major PoS cryptocurrency to officially provide a service like this.

RH: How is the Social X Whitepaper coming along?

Laudney: In the cryptocurrency world, there is this unwritten convention of "releasing whitepaper first, code second". I personally followed that convention for the PoSV announcement and release. But recently I've started to think about why this convention came to existence and whether it's helpful and my conclusion is quite interesting. What are the benefits of releasing a whitepaper early for an open-source project? There are several. First, to establish the precedence of the idea. Second, to gather feedback. Third, to recruit people to work together on the implementation. When it comes to my Social X whitepaper, all these benefits are dwarfed by the risk of giving away too much of our game plan too early to competitors. If you think about it, no company releases details of their upcoming new products long before they are actually able to ship those products. It's almost ludicrous to give away technical specifications and vision before seizing the first-mover advantage in the market place and dealing a blow to competitors with element of surprise.

Based on this reasoning, I've been focusing on writing code and the whitepaper in parallel and plan to release the whitepaper when implementation is largely finished.

RH: So you're already working on the code - exciting to hear! One last quick question for you: do you do a lot of reading? Who are your favourite authors?

Laudney: Yes. Reading is part of my daily routine. My favourite authors are Carl Sagan and Neil Stephenson.

PROOF OF STAKE VELOCITY
DESIGN WHITE PAPER
PUBLISHED IN APRIL 2014

Proof of Stake Velocity: Building the Social Currency of the Digital Age

Larry Ren*

ren@reddcoin.com

www.reddcoin.com

April 2014

Abstract

Proof of Stake Velocity (PoSV) is proposed as an alternative to Proof of Work (PoW) and Proof of Stake (PoS) to secure the peer-to-peer network and confirm transactions of Reddcoin, a cryptocurrency created specifically to facilitate social interactions in the digital age. PoSV is designed to encourage both ownership (Stake) and activity (Velocity) which directly correspond to the two main functions of Reddcoin as a real currency: store of value and medium of exchange. Reddcoin can also function as the unit of account in heterogeneous social context. The technological aspects of PoSV are presented after a detailed review of existing designs. The economic aspects of Reddcoin are then analysed. Finally the unique position of Reddcoin as a digital social currency in the competitive landscape of cryptocurrencies is discussed.

1 Introduction

Bitcoin is among today's most discussed and controversial topics. Ever since Satoshi's seminal paper [9] in 2008, Bitcoin has evolved from a technological experiment embraced by a small group of computer enthusiasts to what some today consider to be the most important innovation since Internet. Most recently, there are new variants of Bitcoin, called *altcoins*, created everyday and a whole new industry of altcoin trading exchanges, mining pools, gaming websites emerged. Few topics today are more polarising than cryptocurrency. Some merits of cryptocurrency touted by technologists are considered sins by economists. Cryptocurrency is considered a movement by believers and a fad by disbelievers. Instead of an open and honest discussion involving all sides, what we have witnessed is a dialogue of the deaf, in which each camp justifies its own intellectual laziness by pointing to the intellectual laziness of the other camps. This is one

---

* The lead developer of Reddcoin, a.k.a. "laudney" PGP Public Key

1

of the main obstacles that prevent cryptocurrency from being accepted by the general public.

What do we really know about this evolution? Is cryptocurrency just a technological breakthrough or also an economic one [7]? Is *mining* cryptocurrency a progress or retrogression [6]? Is cryptocurrency meant to replace government and financial institutions or complement them? Is cryptocurrency designed for hoarding or spending? And, the most fundamental question of all: is cryptocurrency real currency or just virtual property for speculation [23]?

So far innovation in the cryptocurrency world has been almost exclusively technical. Technologists have proposed improvement on various aspects of Bitcoin, such as new hash functions [11] to replace SHA256 and new mechanism [4] to replace Proof-of-Work. There have been very few cryptocurrencies designed to address the economic and social aspects of being a real currency. Reddcoin, at the time of writing, seems to be only one.

We write this paper with three goals in mind: 1) to give a broad overview of the current issues around cryptocurrency, both technological and economic, which might not have been foreseen by the original designers. 2) to address these issues with proposals which require coordinated changes in both low-level network protocol and high-level economic and social ecosystem. 3) to encourage a more open and objective discussion of cryptocurrency by the general public and promote a more complete thinking for future innovation in cryptocurrency world.

The rest of the paper is organised as follows. Section 2 describes in detail the merits and drawbacks of Proof-of-Work (PoW) and Proof-of-Stake (PoS) from both technological and economic points of view. PoSV is then proposed to address those drawbacks in the specific context of a digital social currency. The technological design choices of PoSV are given in broad strokes. More detailed technical analyses will be presented in a companion paper [12]. Section 3 addresses the most common criticisms by economists on cryptocurrency and shows how Reddcoin and PoSV together provide new answers and new opportunities for social research in general. Section 4 emphasises the main differences between Reddcoin, a digital social currency which focuses on integration with human social interactions and aims to concretise and quantify people's intangible asset of social influence, and the much more common digital commercial currencies which aim to facilitate transactions of goods and services and offer protection from hyperinflation.

2   Technology

A cryptocurrency uses principles of cryptography to implement a distributed, decentralised and secure cash system. It solves the problem of double-spending in a distributed ledger by introducing a mechanism to secure the network against 51% attacks and Distributed Denial of Service (DDoS) attacks. The underlying principle of such a mechanism is the necessity of expending resources when confirming transactions. Once confirmed, transactions become irreversible because it's practically infeasible for any attacker to have access to the huge amount of resource required to modify them. Different mechanisms use different types of resources.

2.1 Proof of Work

A Proof-of-Work (PoW) is a piece of data which is costly to produce so as to satisfy certain requirements but is trivial to verify. Bitcoin uses the Hashcash PoW [ ]. Mining, the process of producing PoW, plays the central role in creating, distributing and securing Bitcoin and many its variants. The most common criticism of PoW mining is its massive waste of energy. At the time of writing, the total daily revenue of mining Bitcoin is around 1.8 million USD. Depending on the aggregate profit margin and the fraction of overall cost that electricity accounts for, we estimate the daily total electricity cost at between 200K and 500K USD. In addition to this wastefulness, there are several more reasons why mining remains a very controversial aspect of PoW cryptocurrencies.

2.1.1 Mining Arms Race

Mining is by nature extremely competitive. Mining costs include initial expenditure on equipment plus on-going energy cost. Miners are predominantly rational profit seekers. Their top concern is how long it takes to recover the initial cost, i.e. the length of Return on Investment (ROI). During the very early age of Bitcoin, mining was carried out by CPU. When mining later became available on graphics cards (GPU), mining on CPU became immediately loss-making. As Bitcoin price continued to soar, mining operation witnessed a mini industrial revolution. Application Specific Integrated Circuit (ASIC) designed to carry out PoW computation at several magnitude higher speed and lower energy cost started to emerge and soon rendered GPU mining obsolete. This relentless arms race causes constant worry among average miners who usually fail to recuperate initial investment and cannot afford continuous hardware upgrade.

Bitcoin uses SHA256 [10] as the hash function in PoW and is the first to experience this arms race. The same arms race is happening to cryptocurrencies that use the Scrypt hash function [11]. Scrypt was initially touted as "ASIC-resistant" due to its heavier memory usage. In reality, ASIC-resistance is one of the most misleading and over-abused marketing slogans in the cryptocurrency world. The correct word is "ASIC-ignored". ASIC can be designed and manufactured to perform all hash functions. The entry barrier is not technical but financial. Unless there is sufficient market demand for mining Scrypt-based cryptocurrencies, it's simply financially unprofitable for manufacturers to invest in the production of such ASICs. While Scrypt is under the threat of ASIC, many cryptocurrencies have been created to use alternative hash functions such as Scrypt-N, Scrypt-Jane and X11. These cryptocurrencies all market themselves as the "latest and best generation of" ASIC-resistance when this resistance is entirely dependent on being a minority. It's deeply self-contradictory

3

for a cryptocurrency to pitch ASIC-resistance as its main merit to gain wide adoption when this sole merit depends on it being unpopular.

In theory, it can be preferable to have separation between mining a cryptocurrency and using it. It's more efficient to leave mining operation to specialists who use their domain knowledge to achieve economy of scale. This is indeed the case for Bitcoin, the most established cryptocurrency. However, for many newly created variants, average GPU-miners make up the vast majority of user communities and the fear of ASIC directly threatens their social fabric.

2.1.2 Miner Incentive

Miners provide a paid service to cryptocurrency networks. They are all profit seekers first and foremost. At a fixed cost, it's perfectly rational for them to mine the most profitable cryptocurrency and sell it quickly on market to limit exposure to price risks. Hence were born the so-called "multipools" which fully automate this process. Multipools create two new problems in the cryptocurrency world.

First, the profit-seeking by multipools pushes many cryptocurrency prices to just above mining production cost. As mining production costs inevitably go down due to technological advances, many cryptocurrency prices suffer from downward death spiral, which hurts the morale of the corresponding communities. Second, multipools employ strategies that exploit the lag in readjustment of difficulty of PoW. Multipools switch to a cryptocurrency with low difficulty and keep mining it while its difficulty gradually catches up. The moment the difficulty rises to its fair value, multipools switch again. As a consequence, multipools mine blocks at a significantly lower average difficulty than other miners. Although from a pure Darwinian point of view multipools help improve market efficiency and filter out the weakest, they do force most cryptocurrencies to focus on extremely short-term interests rather than long-term growth and innovation.

2.1.3 Manufacturers of ASIC Mining Equipment

To be the most profitable miner, one must be the first to get hold of the latest equipment that offers the highest hash rate per unit of cost. Therefore manufacturers of ASIC mining equipment have strong financial incentive to use their own product for mining first and only start shipping equipment to buyers after mining profitability drops enough. This inherent conflict of interests has profound impact on every aspect of the mining business. For example, the vast majority of manufacturers ask for prepayment in exchange for a promise. The actual delivery is usually delayed by months, which reduces mining profitability for their buyers to almost zero. Manufacturers often offer no refund for shipping delay or product defect in their terms and conditions, effectively eliminating their own liabilities and openly exploiting the desperation of buyers. All these frustrations reduce the confidence of average miners and undermine the soundness of PoW mining as the guardian of cryptocurrencies' decentralised networks.

4

2.2 Proof of Stake

Proof-of-Stake (PoS) is an alternative to PoW first introduced in Peercoin [4]. The resource used by PoS is "coin age": currency amount times holding period. Similar to energy, coin age as a resource is expensive to amass in huge quantity. For an attacker to accumulate enough coin age to attack the distributed network, he either has to buy on open market a large amount of the very currency he's trying to attack, driving up its price during the process and diminishing his economic incentive, or hold coins for a very long time, reducing the frequency of his own attacks.

One useful feature of PoS is the significant saving in energy consumption. Another main feature is the better alignment of incentives between miners and stakeholders because miners are now the stakeholders. PoS however has several limitations:

2.2.1 Initial Distribution

PoS by construction relies on a fair and wide distribution of a cryptocurrency but doesn't deal with the *logistical* issue of how to achieve this fair distribution in the first place. By comparison, mining in PoW, despite all its drawbacks, also serves as a potent channel of distribution. This chicken-and-egg problem was and remains a major challenge for all PoS cryptocurrencies. So far there have been two popular workarounds: a) "pre-mine", i.e. similar to subscription to stock IPO in financial markets and b) a hybrid system of PoW and PoS with PoW gradually fading away after an initial period.

The main criticism of "pre-mine" for PoS coins is its lack of guarantee of either fair or wide adoption. The vast majority of "pre-mine" turned out to be fraud. For those which were not, investors and speculators with deep pockets can easily control a large stake in the currency, transforming its nature into more as a speculative vehicle than a currency. Over-concentration of stakes also increases the security risk of the decentralised network.

The PoW-PoS hybrid system alleviates these concerns by running PoW and PoS in parallel. PoW mining works as both a steady distribution channel and a fall-back network security mechanism. As PoW block rewards go down over time, PoS has enough time to move to the spotlight.

Unfortunately, it doesn't matter what particular model a PoS cryptocurrency uses for initial distribution. The mere knowledge by the public that a cryptocurrency will eventually rely on PoS compromises its ability to achieve a fair and wide distribution. This is the inherent paradox of Proof-of-Stake.

2.2.2 Hoarding

The entire PoS network depends on coin age as the scarce resource. Coin age can only be earned by holding coins. To earn coin age at a higher rate than others, one must hold more coins. Coin age is consumed when a coin is spent in a transaction. PoS mining requires a user to repeatedly send coins to herself, thus consuming his reserve of coin age in exchange for probabilistic winning

5

a PoS block reward without reducing the size of the holding. Coins spent in transactions facing other users also have their coin age reset to zero but this consumption of coin age is outside the scope of PoS mining, unqualified for block rewards and is considered a "waste" by most PoS stakeholders.

It now becomes clear that PoS has been designed to encourage hoarding and discourage spending. Some PoS coins, such as Peercoin, openly declare their philosophy to "function more as a long-term store of value than medium of exchange." In this sense, PoS coins are created to be *collectibles* rather than currencies. Scarcity is a necessary but insufficient condition for collectibles to have value. Collectibles must also offer some form of utility such as aesthetics and historic significance. Considering the fact that anyone can access and modify the source code of PoS coins and potentially offer an improved version, in theory there is infinite supply. The scarcity condition doesn't hold. It remains an unsolved puzzle where PoS coins marketed as collectibles derive their value from.

2.2.3 Full Nodes

PoS transforms all stakeholders into miners. All they need to do to collect interest rate is to leave their wallets running and connected to the PoS network and participate in the confirmation of transactions. Wallets which stay online for extended periods of time are called *full nodes*. Staying online seems to be a rather simple requirement. So it comes as quite a surprise that PoS coins tend to suffer from insufficient number of full nodes. This seeming paradox can be explained by two reasons.

First, coin age equals number of coins times holding period. It doesn't matter whether a wallet is connected to the PoS network during the holding period. An offline wallet accumulates coin age at the same rate as an online one. The only difference is that an always-online wallet receives block rewards in a fashion that's more evenly spread out over time while an occasionally-online wallet receives block rewards in a few concentrated clusters. This difference alone is insufficient to encourage most stakeholders to stay online.

Second, it's commonly perceived by average PoS stakeholders that running wallets and staying connected for long periods of time significantly increases security risk. This was a particularly grave concern when early versions of PoS wallets didn't support wallet passphrase during mining. Since then there has been workaround to reduce the security risk.

By considering the two reasons above, an average PoS stakeholder tend to make the rational decision of connecting to PoS network only sporadically. The lack of sufficient number of full nodes can result in higher risk of security breach on PoS networks.

2.2.4 Mining on Multiple Forks

In PoS mining, each stakeholder spends coin age while looking for the next valid block. If another stakeholder finds a valid block first, the coin age consumed in

6

the unsuccessful attempt is fully reimbursed.

Forks do happen on all distributed networks of cryptocurrencies. PoW addresses this issue by enforcing at protocol level that the blockchain with the largest sum of difficulty always wins. This allows all the nodes on the network to converge on a consensus rapidly. Miners all have the clear incentive to mine blocks only for the most difficult blockchain. Mining for any other fork is almost guaranteed to be wasteful. The situation is very different when it comes to PoS.

When there are multiple forks on a PoS network, by the nature of the blockchain, a stakeholder has the same stake replicated across all the forks. Technically the stakeholder can simultaneously mine on all these forks by running multiple copies of the wallet. What causes the biggest trouble is the fact that PoS protocol picks a winning blockchain based on length. And length of a blockchain in a decentralised network heavily depends on timing. It can be quite common for different subsets of the network to have different ideas about which blockchain is the longest while the information is still being propagated. The lack of synchronisation of network time further complicates it. It's a much less robust way, compared to PoW, to reach a consensus. PoS can't use the sum of difficulty in blockchains as the criteria for chain selection because difficulty in PoS is adjusted by each stakeholder based on their consumption of coin age and therefore remains local knowledge. There is no network-wide agreed-upon block difficulty.

When stakeholders on PoS networks find it difficult to pick the blockchain winner, they have the incentive to "bet on all horses" by simultaneously mining on all the forks. This significantly aggravates network security. Most PoS coins alleviate, but don't solve, this problem by enforcing "duplicate stake detection" at client wallet level but not at protocol level. They also argue that in practice the financial rewards for multi-fork miners are small enough to deter such attempts.

2.3 Proof of Stake Velocity

2.3.1 What is Velocity of Money

The velocity of money is the frequency at which one unit of currency flows through an economy while being used by members of the society within a given time period [3]. All else being equal, a higher velocity of money indicates a more flourishing economy, richer members and a healthier financial system. The formula to measure velocity of money in a given time frame is the follow:

$$V_T = \frac{nT}{M}$$

where V_T is the velocity of money; nT is the aggregate notional of transactions and M is total amount of money in circulation. In an economy, we can also replace nT with nQ which is the nominal national or domestic product. In other words, given a fixed amount of money in circulation, velocity of money must be increased in order to increase the size of the economy.

7

2.3.2 Higher Velocity for A Better Economy

The vast majority of the drawbacks of PoW and PoS aren't due to flaws in technical designs but the disconnect from the *economic* and *social* aspects of being a real currency. It's fair to say that most cryptocurrencies are created as technological products but "mis-sold" as currencies. PoSV builds upon the strength of PoS and introduces new features to address its flaws. PoSV is designed to encourage both ownership (Stake) and activity (Velocity), the two main criteria of being a social currency. It must be emphasised that PoSV is designed specifically for the digital social currency *Reddcoin* and is never intended to serve as a drop-in replacement for other cryptocurrencies that don't share the same economic and social goals. PoSV should be evaluated as a piece in the Reddcoin ecosystem and not stand-alone.

Given a fixed amount of coin, coin age is calculated as a function of time. Let's denote this function the *coin-aging function*. The form of the coin-aging function is of ultimate importance. It not only decides the growth rate of coin age as a resource over time via its first derivative, but also decides the *utility function* of stakeholders. The main limitations of PoS, too much incentive for hoarding and too little incentive for staying online, result from the fact that the form of its coin-aging function is linear. The linear form leads to a constant coin age growth rate and a utility function that disobeys the law of diminishing returns.

Changing the form of coin-aging function has profound impact. For example, let's assume coin-aging function in PoSV is an exponential decay function. The coin age growth rate gradually decreases with time. The exponential decay constant is chosen to achieve a particular half-life such as 1 month. Each coin accumulates one coin day per calendar day during the first month, half a coin day per calendar day during the second month, a fourth of a coin day per calendar day during the third month etc. As the holding period of a coin approaches infinity, the total accumulated coin age asymptotically approaches 2 coin months.

This exponential decay function dramatically changes stakeholders' incentives. New coin accumulates coin age at much higher rate than stale ones. With a fine-tuned half-life, PoSV encourages stakeholders to be *active* in moving their holding, either by mining or transacting with counterparties, both of which increase money velocity and improve the health of the Reddcoin economy. Stakeholders are also encouraged to stay online and contribute to verifying transactions on the PoSV network. The asymptotic limit of coin age due to exponential decay function provides extra security for the network. The maximum amount of coin age a stakeholder can earn now equals coin amount times twice the half-life. This significantly increases the difficulty for 51% attacks.

The coin-aging function can take on other forms. Linear and exponential decay functions are both monotonic. What about trigonometric functions which are non-monotonic and periodic? Non-monotonicity produces positive and negative growth rate of coin age at different points in time which along with periodicity translate into rewarding and penalising holding with a seasonal pattern.

8

This can be used to fine-tune the seasonality in money velocity. The bottom line is that PoSV is designed to accommodate different forms of coin-aging functions in order to implement the necessary monetary policies in the Reddcoin economy.

To alleviate the problem of mining on multiple forks, PoSV helps the nodes to reach a quicker consensus by giving preference to the head block with the largest sum of coin day spent among all the transactions.

3 Economics

There has been extensive economics debate about Bitcoin. Most economists remain unconvinced of Bitcoin's status as a real currency. Reddcoin and PoSV are designed to address some of those concerns and offer new angles to reexamine the questions.

3.1 Medium of Exchange

There is largely consensus on Bitcoin's function as a medium of exchange. In fact, almost all the merits of Bitcoin talked about today boil down to how it acts as a better medium of exchange, e.g. global reach, lower fees, much quicker transaction and easy to use. However, the fact that the Bitcoin network must be secured by "mining" which expends real resources (energy) is considered by many economists to be a drastic retrogression [0] - a retrogression that Adam Smith scorned at in his immortal work *The Wealth of Nations* written in 1776. By comparison, PoSV and PoS mining require little energy consumption and can be done by any average user on any computer and even mobile device.

3.2 Unit of Account

Many economists point out that Bitcoin cannot be used as the base currency for accounting or tax-reporting and therefore fails as a unit of account. Interestingly, the german finance ministry has officially classified Bitcoin as a unit of account. More and more merchants start to accept Bitcoin for payment. Especially in the world of cryptocurrencies, Bitcoin has assumed the special status of a *reserve currency* and is the choice of denomination for more and more goods and services. Reddcoin and PoSV bring a whole new question: what is the "unit of account" for human social interactions, if any?

Currently social interactions are quantified in different ways on different social networks. On Facebook, it may be measured in the number of *Like* and *Share*; on Twitter, the number of *retweets*; on Amazon, the number and quality of product reviews; on blogs and forums, the number of posts and replies. The total lack of a universal yardstick makes it impossible to measure and compare social interactions in heterogenous context. In other words, there is no unit of account for human social interactions right now. Social influence remains a significant yet opaque asset.

9

Reddcoin is created to fill this gap by becoming the first digital currency integrated with all major social networks and serving as the "unit of account" for social interactions in the digital age. Inside the distributed ledger of Reddcoin, transactions can be interpreted not only in pure financial terms but also as proxies for human behaviours. Researchers in social sciences have long been looking for a way to track, organise and study human social behaviours on large scales. Reddcoin offers a unique global platform for these areas of research and open up new possibilities for value-add services.

3.3   Store of Value

Economists are largely skeptical of Bitcoin's function as a store of value. They compare Bitcoin with gold and US dollars and point out its lack of a fundamental floor of the value [2]:

> Underpinning the value of gold is that if all else fails you can use it to make pretty things. Underpinning the value of the dollar is a combination of (a) the fact that you can use them to pay your taxes to the U.S. government, and (b) that the Federal Reserve is a potential dollar sink and has promised to buy them back and extinguish them if their real value starts to sink at (much) more than 2% per year. Placing a floor on the value of Bitcoins is what, exactly?

PoSV, PoW or PoS by itself doesn't provide a fundamental floor for the value of a cryptocurrency. However, Reddcoin, the digital social currency that PoSV is specifically designed for, does enjoy a floor of its value due to its aim to function as the global reserve currency of human social influence. Humans are by nature social animals. Social activities are embedded into the very fabric of societies. As Aristotle famously pointed out in *Politics*:

> Society is something that precedes the individual. Anyone who either cannot lead the common life or is so self-sufficient as not to need to, and therefore does not partake of society, is either a beast or a god.

Based on Aristotle's insight, underpinning the value of Reddcoin is simply its utility of helping humans be human.

3.4   Deflation vs Inflation

Any discussion of monetary system is incomplete without discussing inflation. Bitcoin and many of its variants were created with a deflation model in which the total quantity of the cryptocurrency is capped. In effect, Bitcoin has created a modern digital version of the gold standard world in which the money supply is fixed rather than subject to increase via printing press.

10

Bitcoin advocates believe deflation is a virtue by preserving the value of Bitcoin versus inflationary fiat currencies and thus making it a better store of value. Bitcoin price has indeed soared in the last few years, further validating the merit of deflation in its supporters' mind.

However, deflation and a soaring price both provide strong incentives for people to hoard Bitcoin rather than spending it. Indeed, according to [ ], as much as 64% of Bitcoin was never spent in 2013. To make matters worse, prices of goods and services when measured in Bitcoin have plunged; the Bitcoin economy has in effect suffered a major depression [ ].

PoS and PoSV both employ an inflation model with fixed nominal interest rate. For example Peercoin adopts a nominal interest rate of 1% per annum compared to PoSV's 5%. Central banks in developed countries, e.g. Bank of England, European Central Bank and Federal Reserve, have a long-term inflation target of around 2%. PoSV chooses 5% because Reddcoin, as the digital social currency, should encourage more spending, i.e. social interactions, than other cryptocurrencies which do not share this goal. Also given the global nature of social networks which involve users in both developed and emerging markets, 5% seems to strike the balance. The monetary system of Reddcoin is not created to make people who hold money rich, but to facilitate transactions and make the Reddcoin economy as a whole rich.

4 Digital Social Currency

4.1 Social vs Commercial

A commercial currency is the most common form of currency. Its main function is to facilitate transactions in exchange for goods and services. Bitcoin and its variants have been pushed as the latest innovation of commercial currencies and compete head-to-head with fiat currencies, such as USD and EUR, for shares of commercial transactions in the global economy.

A social currency is of an entirely different nature. According to Wikipedia:

> Social currency is a common term that can be understood as the entirety of actual and potential resources which arise from the presence in social networks and communities, may they be digital or offline. It derives from Pierre Bourdieu's social capital theory and is about increasing one's sense of community, granting access to information and knowledge, helping to form one's identity, and providing status and recognition.

Very recently, a small but growing number of companies have come to embrace the concept of "social currency", allowing customers to pay via Facebook posts, Twitter tweets and other social media content. However the lack of a yardstick to measure the "fair value" of social media content and influence is the main obstacle. To our knowledge, Reddcoin is the only digital social currency

11

that was created, designed and continuously evolves to become the "reserve currency" of people's social interactions. Reddcoin has two main objectives: 1) to concretise and quantify one's intangible asset of social influence, and 2) to facilitate social interactions within and between social networks, both online and offline. Reddcoin doesn't compete with commercial currencies, fiat or digital, but rather complement them. Merchant support is encouraged, especially when the commercial activities form parts of a collective social experience. But the social aspect will always remain the utmost focus of Reddcoin.

The three most important assets in the ecosystem of Reddcoin are brand, community and infrastructure. Reddcoin developers always go to great length to create a brand that's professional, friendly and consistent. Great care is taken to foster a community that share a clear long-term mission and the same set of values of being friendly, helpful, generous, caring and rational. All system infrastructure is built with special emphasis on providing a uniform, simple and secure user experience.

4.2 Transition from PoW to PoSV

Reddcoin was launched in January 2014 and is still using PoW. Since the very beginning, Reddcoin has been distributed to a large and diverse user base through multiple channels that include one of the very few successful and honest Initial Public Coin Offering (IPCO), mining, trading on multiple exchanges, community promotion events, generous giveaways and user tipping on multiple social networks such as Reddit, Twitter and Twitch TV. Reddcoin stakeholders now include people from almost 100 countries, with diverse background, age and interests.

At the time of writing, according to information at http://bitinfocharts.com, Reddcoin has a fairer wealth distribution per wallet address than all the top cryptocurrencies such as Bitcoin, Litecoin, Dogecoin and Peercoin. Reddcoin also has 2 - 3 times more coin age spent today than all the other PoW cryptocurrencies. Reddcoin, without PoSV, is already the currency with the fairest stake ownership and the highest monetary velocity. In coming months, Reddcoin will gradually transition from PoW to PoSV with new features added at incremental pace.

4.3 Hard to Clone

There is no shortcut to cloning Reddcoin. In particular, the clone cannot adopt PoSV from inception because, as discussed in section 2, the mere knowledge of the eventual adoption of PoSV or PoS will lead to people hoarding from the very beginning. To achieve a fair and wide distribution, an element of surprise at protocol level plus dedicated efforts at community level are both indispensable. Reddcoin's existing brand, community, infrastructure and the publication of this paper make it very difficult to duplicate what has already been achieved.

12

5   Conclusion

We have proposed Proof-of-Stake-Velocity (PoSV) as an alternative to Proof-of-Work (PoW) and Proof-of-Stake (PoS). We started by going through all the major drawbacks of PoW and PoS and then showed how PoSV significantly reduces the wastefulness of mining, eliminates mining arms race, averts the threat of multipools and ASICs, avoids the inherent conflict of interests by ASIC manufacturers, introduces new forms of coin-aging functions to discourage hoarding and encourage spending and greater contribution to the network. General concerns by economists toward cryptocurrency were discussed and addressed in light of the recent development of Reddcoin and PoSV. In particular, Reddcoin is well positioned to fill the niche of a digital social currency that's tightly integrated with human social interactions and acts as the yardstick to concretise and quantify people's intangible asset of social influence.

References

[1] Adam Back. Hashcash - A Denial of Service Counter-Measure. 2002.

[2] Brad DeLong. Watching Bitcoin, Dogecoin Etc... 2013.

[3] Joshua Kennon. The Velocity of Money for Beginners. 2012.

[4] Sunny King and Scott Nadal. PPCoin: Peer-to-Peer Crypto-Currency with Proof-of-Stake. 2012.

[5] Paul Krugman. Golden Cyberfetters. 2013.

[6] Paul Krugman. Adam Smith Hates Bitcoin. 2013.

[7] Paul Krugman. An Ubernerd Weighs In. 2013.

[8] Sarah Meiklejohn, Marjori Pomarole, Grant Jordan, Kirill Levchenko, Damon McCoy, Geoffrey M. Voelker, and Stefan Savage. A Fistful of Bitcoins: Characterizing Payments Among Men with No Names. *Internet Measurement Conference*, 2013.

[9] Satoshi Nakamoto. Bitcoin: A Peer-to-Peer Electronic Cash System. 2008.

[10] National Institute of Standards and Technology. Secure Hash Standard (SHS). 2012.

[11] Colin Percival. Stronger Key Derivation via Sequential Memory-hard Functions. 2012.

[12] Larry Ren. Proof-of-Stake-Velocity: Technical Analyses. to appear.

[13] David Yermack. Is Bitcoin a Real Currency? An economic appraisal. 2013.

13

reddcoin
roadmap

Social Tip Platform

Utilizes a different protocol from conventional TipBots and integrates directly with reddcoin Social Wallet to allow seamless social tipping across all major social networks. (Q4 2014)

Social Wallet

State-of-the-art wallet that provides various social features to increase engagement among reddcoin users & to facilitate social tipping. (August 2014)

We are Here

A

PoSV Launch

Proof-of-Stake-Velocity solves known problems in Proof-of-Work & Proof-of-Stake algorithms by encouraging ownership(Stake) & activity(Velocity). (August 02, 2014)

PoSV 2.0

More innovation to further
encourage ownership(Stake)
and activity(Velocity).

Social Broadcast

Reddcoin Broadcast will evolve into Social Broadcast
to provide powerful marketing tools to businesses
and steady reddcoin income to individuals based
on their social influence level.
(Q4 2014)

Social X

Top secret project.
Whitepaper to be revealed
in early September.
(September 2014)

www.ingramcontent.com/pod-product-compliance
Lightning Source LLC
Chambersburg PA
CBHW070858180526
45168CB00005B/1864